THE SAVVY ENTREPRENEUR

An Insider's Secrets to Managing For Success

Our doubts are traitors and make us lose the good
we oft might win by fearing to attempt

—*William Shakespeare*
Measure for Measure

Linda ~
Great to be
in touch again
Best, Lee

THE SAVVY ENTREPRENEUR
An Insider's Secrets to Managing For Success.

Inquiries should be directed in writing to
leepryor@interventuresllc.com
www.interventuresllc.com

ISBN 0-9763465-6-7

Cover Illustration by: PM Graphics

Printed in the United States of America

Attention Colleges and Universities, Professional Organizations and Associations: Quantity discounts are available on bulk purchases of this book for educational or gift purchases.

To my wife Julie Smith, who has encouraged
me to tell the stories and chronicle the experiences.
Her support, encouragement and inspiration in this as in all
undertakings goes way beyond the mark.

Contents

Acknowledgments

I was fortunate to have Lloyd Dobyns spend untold hours editing my manuscript. Also Lloyd's no nonsense approach, combined with his years of experience as an NBC News reporter and correspondent, helped me with content suggestions when I was most assuredly going awry.

This book could not have been written with-out his help!

When an entrepreneur turns to writing, a disaster could be in the making, so the encouragement of my wife, Julie Smith, and the advice and assistance of Bill Pryor, John Pryor, Thalia Pryor and Tor Solberg, has been more than helpful.

To Kit Wohl, for leading me to Lloyd Dobyns, to Tony Cook, and to the many other friends and business associates who have encouraged me to put this all down, thanks again!

THE SAVVY ENTREPRENEUR
An Insider's Secrets to Managing For Success

Introduction

Starting a new business and managing one that is growing quickly is one of the more important things a person can do. You usually get only one chance at it, so it is critical to have all the knowledge you can get about doing it right.

This book is about managing start-ups and small-to-medium size companies. It's for the people who start them, run them, and invest in them.

This book is not intended for Mom and Pop businesses unless there is a sparkle in your eye to expand your business.

It is written to help entrepreneurs and managers of growing enterprises recognize *management* practices that make start-ups as well as small-and-medium size businesses grow into successful, profitable companies.

Entrepreneurship is in some ways like parenthood; these two critical endeavors typically get less formal training than a McDonald's burger slinger. The attempt here is to help with the first of these; not the second one.

My knowledge comes from the first-hand experience of founding and running a successful start-up, which grew to $48 million in sales, and then managing, over a period of years, six small-to-medium size, growing entrepreneurial businesses.

After running a few of them, I began to see similar management patterns. This book covers the many *successful* and *unsuccessful* management practices

I've witnessed during a career-long adventure in the world of entrepreneurship.

The methodology, where applicable, is to briefly recount experiences I've had in order to bring to life behavior, conduct, and practices, that, when taken together, can make a huge difference.

To some, my occasional anecdotes may seem difficult to believe. To others, the stories and management practices related here might seem all too familiar.

I would hope that taking several hours to read this book will help most entrepreneurs manage their companies more successfully starting tomorrow morning.

For others, the shadow of the memory of these anecdotes and practices may surface years later to assist you.

Small companies are hard as hell to run. Start-ups are even harder.

Many never make it through to profitability.

It seems to me, with a firm grip on the obvious, that there are really only four reasons for not making it:

- Bad management.
- Invalid business strategy.
- Flawed product.
- Lack of working capital.

This book concentrates on management practices because if you can't manage your business successfully, you really don't have a business of any value no matter how brilliant your strategy, how wonderful your product, or how many buckets of other people's money you have accumulated.

I have to say that a close second to bad management as a cause for failure is a flawed business strategy. Not just a business plan; but the entire enchilada formulata.

Several important comments about business strategy come later, since if it is flawed, the best jockey in the world can have big trouble trying to turn a nag into a thoroughbred.

One can talk about "sea changes," "synergies," and "paradigm shifts" all day long. But a really savvy entrepreneur builds a successful company by recognizing that there is no one large overwhelming secret to success.

Even though statistics say the most common reason for not making it is running out of money, if you really have a valid profit strategy and manage your company well, you will probably not run out of willing investors.

I learned the importance of many of the practices mentioned in this book by making numerous mistakes on my own; didn't need anyone's help; but I believe I learned from each mistake and now pass on that education to those who care to learn.

As a wise person said, "You will make mistakes if you attempt to do anything at all: it's just best not to make the same mistake twice."

While thinking about writing this book I reflected on the many questions, challenges, and problems I had heard from my peer CEOs or wannabe entrepreneurs during my 30 years of entrepreneurial experiences. I had spent many years in YPO (Young Presidents Organization) and I had spoken to many entrepreneurial and venture capital groups, and participated in numerous management discussions and seminars.

Besides my own experiences, what was I hearing over time that I could put into writing to help others better manage their companies?

First of all, my reflections told me that there were not just several, but a whole host of issues that concerned in-the-trenches entrepreneurs. No one issue seemed to dominate. As one might suspect, different individuals had different problems or challenges at different times. But they mostly revolved around people and management issues.

Therefore, my approach here is to cover most of the important management practices that I have either seen or heard others talk about. In order to cover this many important management topics, I have had to keep my comments brief and to the point. Many topics are supplemented with anecdotes to bring them to life, while some are worthy of an entire book.

You can choose the chapters that may interest you most; however, for you to become a completely well trained-entrepreneur--- an oxymoron I attempt to remedy--- you should of course read the entire book.

If you are one who is thinking about starting a business, you may, before reading this book, want to read Section XI titled "Is Entrepreneurship for Me?".

For those who pass the test and decide to embark on an adventure in entrepreneurship, the practices outlined in this book should prove valuable for you.

For those who already have embarked on the voyage, this book can serve as an invaluable tutorial and reference to the "best practices" which, if followed, will lead you to outrageous success.

That's it then: good strategy, superior product idea, available capital, and most important of all, good management.

And that starts with you!

PART ONE

THE COMPANY CULTURE

Establishing your company culture early on is critical to success. There is no one discipline that defines the company culture. Success is insured by practicing a number of cultural imperatives. Nine of the most important are discussed next.

Be Nimble, Be Quick

God so loved the world that he did not send a committee

Nothing like the above quote could so aptly describe the advantage you have as an entrepreneur.

Entrepreneurial companies, which by definition means small to start with, have numerous advantages over large companies that "small" brings to the game.

You can make decisions quickly and implement them.

You can change strategies fast as competition and customers give you the signals that indicate you're going down the wrong path, or the right one.

You need to change pricing on a product?

You can do it four times faster than the managers of a large company, who will still be in a committee meeting trying to run every option known to humankind long after you have started to eat their breakfast.

Do it!

You need to change a production process that can improve productivity by three percent?

You, the plant manager, and the shift foremen can review the pros and cons, make a decision, and get it done in a week. You think a larger facility with a union shop can do that?

You'll leave the big guys mumbling in their martinis.

Do it!

3

You need to let a non-performer go? You'll be doing it 100 times faster than a large company where HR will hold the decision up for decades. You need to give ample warning, and you need to try re-training, so get started and do it right.

But do it!

You want to change the commission structure for sales to emphasize a special push for a product you just introduced? Meet with the sales manager, run the sales objectives, run the pricing numbers, and implement it next week.

You'll leave the big guys stumbling over their wing tips.

Do it!

You need to set up a customer retention action plan and reporting system?

Buy an off-the-shelf proven software package, meet with customer service, accounting, and sales, and then install it in Monday.

You'll leave the big guys with their ties in their soup.

Do it!

You need to survey your customers to see what they think about the delivery and quality of your product or service?

Meet with whoever maintains your website, buy a $450 survey package, install it, and put the questions out there on Friday. You'll be surprised at the response.

You'll leave the big guys' IT departments talking about HTML, ASP, bigger "pipes" and more "boxes" for at least three months. They ain't about to buy a $450 package when they can take six months to invent the wheel, no matter what's wrong with the company's quality and service!

Do it!

The small guy's perception is sometimes that the big guys have all the advantages. They do have many; so your job is to take advantage of the ones you have.

Be nimble, be quick.

Do it!

As Yogi Berra said, "When you come to a fork in a road, take it."

Institutionalize Responsibility and Accountability

Potential is interesting, performance is everything

"With responsibility comes accountability" is one of the most cherished axioms in business. While it gets incredible lip service, my observations have been that in small businesses, it is the most violated of all the important management practices.

I realize what I'm going to recommend next is not quite in tune with the casual approach of most of us entrepreneurs, but the practice is critical to the success of establishing the kind of culture you need for success.

You should have a brief orientation session with each manager the first day they start with the company. You should have a check list or notes on what you want to say to them about working together as a team to establish and maintain a culture for success.

At the top of the list should be the discussion that there are many responsibilities that come with the position, but there is also accountability. Make it clear that meeting objectives, setting an example, motivating and training people, and insuring that the company's goals of customer satisfaction are met are all part of this position's responsibilities.

There are a number of reasons why this orientation meeting is important.

First, you need each manager to understand how important a success culture is to you and to the company's well being.

Second, you need each of them to know that you are depending on them, with you and the other managers, to institutionalize the culture of responsibility and accountability.

Third, you need each of them to understand that practicing responsibility and accountability cannot become an empty chalice.

Responsibility can not be abdicated for the sake of convenience, or to escape from accountability.

You will find that if this culture is set correctly up front, you will see people perform at their best. If you see performance slacking, it will be much easier to have the important conversation that must take place because it will take place in a familiar context.

Once people see you take action on this cultural imperative, you will have put the necessary stamp on it. On the other hand, if you do not take action in a case where objectives have been continually missed where responsibility has been clearly defined, then you lose creditability, and a nail has been driven in the coffin of this extremely important management practice.

Continual excuses for not achieving performance goals agreed upon are the first sign of a problem, so we now move on in the next chapter; dealing with non-performers.

Deal with Non-Performers

Success hath a thousand fathers, failure is but an orphan

Dealing with non-performers is perhaps one of the hardest tasks an entrepreneur has to carry out. Therefore it's the one that's botched far too often, to the detriment of all constituencies, including customers, other employees, and shareholders.

But to foster the culture of accountability, dealing with a non-performer must be faced. Whether it's football, opera, or business, it's all about execution. One non-performer can make the difference between excellence and mediocrity.

In many cases you've hired the person yourself, gotten to know the family, and developed a personal as well as a professional relationship.

Now the person is not performing. It is your job to accept the facts, see it the way it is, and deal with the problem. In almost all cases this process, takes far too long.

You cannot abrogate this responsibility.

I believe, from my own experience, as well as discussions with other entrepreneurs, that the best time to start to face the problem of non-performance is the first minute you think about it!

Not the third month, the first minute!

7

I do not know of a case where after the first time I began worrying about a person's performance, it did not turn out that my gut was right. My problem was that for a long time, I took too long to admit it and address the issue.

After a few signals that a manager is not performing, your gut kicks in and you need to set up an action plan right away.

If they have stolen, cheated, lied, or blatantly violated company policy, call them in and let them go immediately. If they have done any of these things, the right way is the immediate way. Not Friday. Today.

The correct way to let them go, if non-performance is the reason, is to follow this series of steps.

First, when you have that first five-second gut thought about their non-performance, call them in for one of those one-on-one sandwich lunches in your office (discussed in the chapter "Be Available"). During the conversation, remind them of the importance of meeting performance goals. Be specific about recent lapses under their area of responsibility.

Second, discuss the accountability ethic so they know it's on your mind and should be on theirs.

Third, ask what sort of help they need. If it's reasonable, give them the help. If it's not reasonable say no and tell them why. Tell them that you want to see them be successful, and while you'll help as much as is feasible, the successful effort has to come from within. You can not do it for them.

Fourth, if progress is not being made after the first 30 days, it will be evident, so you can then discuss a lateral move for them, if you are big enough to have another position with skill sets more suited to their capability.

Having the lateral-move-possibility discussion will send a huge warning signal to them.

It's like a running back who fumbles too often. The coach pulls him aside and tells him he would probably be more suited to play right tackle! You will unquestionably see a running back who completely stops fumbling as a result of that conversation. I know, because it happened to me and once was enough!

In any case, within 30 to 45 days, you will either witness performance improvement, or if not you will need to take the last step.

Step Five is the process of letting the person go. You should certainly say you hoped that he or she would improve, but that for the good of the company, you have to end it. You will supply a recommendation letter and respond to reference calls.

Be prepared for what is almost invariably the response "How much termination do I get, and what about COBRA benefits?"

I have to tell you a story about the first time I had to come to grips with letting a manager go, because it will hopefully put you at ease about this difficult and unpleasant task.

The company I founded right after leaving IBM grew rapidly from five people and one little garage plant to 55 people and three plants, then to 320 people and five plants, all operating three shifts.

At the three-plant stage we needed a vice president of operations who could handle the many challenges and responsibilities that our multi-plant operation required.

I hired a friend for the position who I knew was bright, detailed, and organized. He had been a Marine aircraft carrier pilot before becoming a product coordinator at Procter and Gamble. He seemed to have all the skills needed to run the operations side of my small but growing company.

After about six months it turned out he did have all the skills, except one: he could not get along well with people, particularly the plant managers who reported to him. I think his high IQ got in the way, but in any case it was clear that he had to go.

I had my-one-on ones with him over the period of several months and still things were not getting better. In fact, the three plant managers had had it with him, which I knew (see the chapter titled "Bottom up Bias").

In any case, when I asked him in my office for another one-on-one lunch, I felt he knew what was coming. I told him we had tried, but it just wasn't working out and I wanted to help him find something else, starting right away.

I expected him to be furious. Instead he asked me what I thought he should do next. After recovering, I told him I thought he was great with numbers and analysis so why didn't he try working for an investment firm where he could be an analyst.

He did just that and became extremely successful. For years he would call me around Christmas and thank me for letting him go!

The moral to this, which should make it easier for you to act quickly with a non- performer, is that everyone has something or someplace where they can excel. If they can't help themselves, you can help them if it isn't working out at your company.

So do it sooner rather than later. It's better for both parties.

Just do it.

See it the Way it is

One of the most egregious failings in our human genome—
whether in business, the military, politics, or our relationship
with another—is when we fail to see it the way it really is

I'll never forget meeting Warren Buffet for the first time.

I flew to Omaha at his request. He had invested in a company that was similar to the company I had started right after leaving IBM, and his company was interested in buying my company.

We met. He seemed an unassuming and no-nonsense kind of guy. It was easy to like him. He said, "Lee, if you sell to us, you can put the money in my fund, still have a job in your company, and you'll have a secure financial future."

I said I would think about it. But I felt I was too young to sell and I knew I was probably too much of an iconoclast to work for anyone but myself. Otherwise why would I have left a potential fast track at IBM to start a company?

We parted with the idea that we would stay in touch. After several more meetings I decided against selling.

What came out of the encounters for me though; especially as the years went by and I followed Buffet's career; was recognizing that Warren, among

11

many excellent qualities, embodies one of the most important characteristics that lead to outstanding success.

He has that rare capacity to see things the way they are.

Warren saw that while I had a decent company, the only way it could become a sizable company was to sell or merge it into a bigger similar company. He saw it the way it was. I saw it the way I wanted to see it. I wanted to continue my entrepreneurial adventure no matter what the logic was for the bigger picture.

He has repeatedly displayed the quality of seeing things the way they are. In fact, the next time I saw him, several years later, was in a hotel elevator in New York City. We rode the elevator down together and then stepped aside into the lobby for a catch-up. He asked what I was doing in New York. I said I was considering taking my company public since the stock market had been doing so well.

He said, "I'd think twice about that, Lee. I'm laying low for a year or two. It just can't continue going up like this."

I stopped my discussions with investment bankers on a public offering and within five weeks the stock market started one of the most precipitous falls ever.

Warren had again seen things the way they really were. And this time I had listened more closely.

My early-in-life encounters with Warren Buffet gave me a reality benchmark, and I've used it for many years. It has served me well. But not as well, by any means, as if I'd sold my company to him back then.

Oh, the price of independence!

As my entrepreneurial journey has progressed, I have recognized, against an evolving palette of encounters with business people, that many of the marginally successful ones share the trait of not seeing things the way they are.

Seeing things the way they are can reveal itself in a macro way, as in the case of Buffet, who did not get involved with the Internet bubble of the late 90s. Or it can manifest itself in micro ways in the challenges and opportunities one encounters every day.

What is the real reason those sales numbers are being missed? Is it the product, is it the sales people, is it a lack of demand, is it the price?

Many executives fall in love with the product and lower the price when that's not the problem. Seeing each facet the way it really is, not the way you hoped or intended it to be, will lead you to a successful decision.

Probably the worst examples of not seeing the things the way they are seem to occur in the development of business strategies that are not based on realities, but instead, are based on wishful thinking.

The Internet boom and bust of the late 1990's was a perfect example. The customers were not ready. Investors and entrepreneurs stuck with the original business plan strategies far after they had proven to be a snare and a delusion. They just would not see things the way they were.

As I say later in this book, it was as if a bunch of investors and entrepreneurs ran around starting United, Delta, and American airlines two years after the Wright Brothers' first flight!

On the other hand, the people at Dell computer saw that the time had come where lap-tops could be sold directly to the customer. The resulting elimination of distribution expenses as an unnecessary burden on the customer allowed them to build an incredibly successful company. They practiced seeing it the way it is, in spades.

See it the way it is!

Forget the Frills

Remember, the little things experienced investors or customers
see immediately about your business, tells them almost all
they need to know about what kind of company you run

The Plant Watering Lady

Ted, a venture capital pal, and I had just come from a quick sushi lunch in downtown Palo Alto. We had met so that he could finish briefing me on his latest potential investment opportunity. He knew I had run a number of companies as an entrepreneur so he asked me if I would take a few hours off and join him while visiting this emerging technology company and its CEO. He wanted to see if I might observe something that could help him with his investment decision.

Over the years of managing emerging technology companies I had kept a developing list of successful management practices learned the hard way, so that I could attempt to improve performance and profitability.

I had learned that you didn't always have to find big things to know a lot about a company, its management and its culture. Many times the little things that are obvious and cannot be hidden are just as revealing. Often it takes no time at all to discover them.

Sort of like a seasoned college football coach. He recognizes talent that first practice day by watching the little things about a player. It's usually hands and heart!

This company was five minutes from the restaurant, so we walked over. We were waiting in the lobby to see the CEO, who was attempting to raise a second round of working capital, when a woman walked through the entrance and started watering the plants in the lobby.

I turned and saw her green plant-watering service van parked in a Reserved for Vice President parking spot out front.

The Plant Watering Lady had on a green smock and was carrying a matching green plastic watering can. Her hair was pulled up and tucked under a green cloth cap.

I turned to Ted and said, "Let's make this a short meeting with the CEO."

Ted muttered, "Are you out of your mind, this company is running out of cash, and I think I can strike a damn good deal. Their industry is just emerging, and everybody wants in."

I said, "Ted, I'm getting some bad culture vibes; let's not waste too much time."

"We've been here four minutes, Lee, and you're beginning to make up your mind. I didn't ask you to come down from San Francisco just so we could jump to conclusions," he said.

"But you did ask me to come down and help you with due diligence on this CEO and how he runs his company, Ted," I said, "and you know what, I don't like the way it's starting out."

Ted said, "We gotta talk later, Pryor."

The CEO took us to his "war room" and showed us the usual Power Point about the industry and the business strategy. A "war room" is a frill I always felt was a bit pretentious for a small company outrunning its cash, particularly when it's full of costly electronic gadgets. How about easel paper taped to the walls instead?

He was an engineer and had an excellent grip on the technology and production side of the business. I had seen these very smart tech types before.

They are usually weak on sales and marketing so I decided to ask more about the sales and marketing plan.

He said that, while he felt the product was so unique that it would practically sell itself, he knew he needed a sales VP and was looking for one. When I asked how long he had been looking and how close he was to finding someone, he said his head-hunter hadn't yet come up with an acceptable candidate.

Head-hunter! The count down for me on frills was already at five; expensive office space in downtown Palo Alto, officers parking next to the front door, plant watering lady, war room, and headhunter. And we had only been there for just over an hour.

On our way back to Ted's office on Sand Hill Road he said, "Well I'm not too sure. I think I need more work on this, but I noticed your first four minute "take" in the lobby was certainly a pre-curser to some questions that I now have about the CEO and several of his plans." Explain your prescience please."

That's when I had to tell Ted my Plant Watering Lady culture detector story.

Years before, on my first assignment to come in and run a troubled second stage start up tech company; on my very first day, with the company bleeding cash and terribly in debt to the banks, I was sitting on my Herman Miller swiveling throne, wondering how to trade the designer desks for Office Depot tables, when in walked, a plant watering lady, green smock, matching watering can, green cap-the whole tortilla.

And this wasn't a Palo Alto company which might be in trouble; this was a Seattle company that was already in deep trouble.

I thought "Holy Macanoli; first it's the fancy furniture and now an outside plant watering service; all in my first three hours. What's next, a King Air at the airport?"

It is amazing what some CEOs will do with other people's money. And it's the little things that tell the tale. It's the little things that form a culture. It's the little things that make a profit.

You can bet the plant watering service in Seattle was discontinued the next day, and that's not the end of that story; more about that company will come later.

Sure enough, those little things pointed to some big problems that took me weeks to discover. If I had not been there every day, 12 hours a day, I would never have discovered the big problems.

Sticking to the thirsty plants. As the years progressed and I went, at the behest of investors, to my second and then third troubled company, there were more plant watering ladies. I couldn't believe it.

My mother once told me she thought I hadn't fallen off the turnip truck more than twice; so it didn't take long for me to develop a culture detector.

Bad cultures make bad companies, and it all starts at the top. You can tell real fast by noticing the little things.

You and I know that having a plant-watering service is far from the only reason for a company not making it. Look at all those successful law firms, banks, and advertising agencies out there in their marble palaces; you can bet there are green smocks all over the place, but that's a different story. More on that later also.

Sure, one plant-watering lady doesn't always make for a failure, but for a start-up or second-stage company, it raises a yellow flag. It's the little things! Watch those frills, little ones and big ones.

Bad frills mean bad culture.

Finishing the Palo Alto Ted story. Because of several other larger concerns, Ted didn't make the investment; and you got it; the Palm Pilot look-alike company was gone in less than two years; after burning through over 12 million dollars of other people's money.

Fortunately, none of Ted's.

Other frills that are absolutely out of line for a start up or a company losing money are: flying first class, limos instead of taxis, ivory tower offices, company loans to officers or directors, expensive company events, and the CEO being over involved in association or community governance. That can all come later; but they are not in the entrepreneurial codebook of cultural success.

I could go on and on with examples of miscreant entrepreneurial behavior; usually with someone else's money. But I'm sure you get the point by now. All frills are not only transparent, they do not add value to the company. While you may think people at the company and the customers don't know about the frills, they do; they all do.

Just forget the frills, at least until you are in deep alfalfa.

Delegate: The Circle Theory

Empowerment breeds achievement

Some time ago I was invited by an important supplier to come to his plant for a visit. He wanted to show me an unusual material handling-system they had installed to lower their cost and increase efficiency to better serve companies like ours.

I had always believed there were many hidden costs in material handling and that it was one of the last places managers went to try to improve service and profitability. I was fascinated by what I saw, but that's another story.

This story is about walking down the hallway to his office where there was a red/green light above his door.

I said, "What's that for?"

He said that he was so busy that, while he didn't like to shut his door, he found he had to so that he wouldn't be interrupted. But then people would just knock and enter anyway, so he put the red/green light over his door and rigged a switch by his desk. If the red light was on, you had better not enter!

Now we all need our private time, but it seemed to me that something was out of control here and that the red light was a symptom. I knew him quite well, as we had been his customer for a long time and had become friends. I even knew that when I called him, his voice mail said that you only had 10

21

seconds to respond. Obviously, this was not only arrogant and condescending, it was another symptom that he had let time management get out of control.

I decided to ask him why he felt he was so damn busy that he needed these mechanisms to save time. He said his company was growing fast and had too many projects going. It was burning all his time just to answer questions and make decisions for people so that things could keep moving.

I asked him if he used the Circle Theory of Managing with his key people. He said he had never heard of it.

I told him I had first thought about it when I was at a circus with my kids and noticed the lion tamer had the lions in a round cage. It seemed to me that most cages are square. The next day I thought about that and made a phone call. The circus Don told me the lions were in a round cage because a square cage would make the big cats think they could hide in a corner.

In any case, here is the Circle Theory of management. And it saves the hell out of your time every day.

You have an annual budget, right? Or if you're a new company you have a business plan.

OK, the plan or budget has everything you are going to do for the fiscal year, right? It has the sales targets, the gross margin target, the marketing budget, the capital expenditures budget, and the personnel hiring plan.

So, you call all of your key people in for your budget wrap-up meeting, which starts on time whether or not they are all there. You review everything in summary form because they, of course, have been the ones who did most of the work in each of the responsible areas.

Then you step to the easel, white board, or cave wall, draw a huge circle and say, "Everything that is in our fiscal year plan we have been reviewing today is inside this circle, got it?"

"All right, please don't come to me for permission to do anything inside the circle. We have already agreed that this is the plan. We have a plan to hire three new sales people in Q2, do it! You don't need me for that or to ask me if we are going to do it, just do it. We have agreed to bring in a new server in Q3. Do it."

"However if you need to go outside the circle and take an action that is not in the circle, that's when we need to talk first. You know we review progress in all of these areas weekly, so we do have a time for discussing changes and adjustments. Plus if you have a major problem you wish to discuss, my door is always open to you but if it's in the circle it's your baby."

"Don't go hide in a corner and don't seek re-affirmation from me."

I wound up my conversation by telling him that operating with this Circle Theory had freed an incredible amount of time for me. More importantly it gave the responsible executives a feeling of ownership and pride, as well as, of course, freeing up the time they felt they had to spend with me!

To control your available time to use for its highest and best use you obviously have to delegate like this, or some better way if you have one.

It's tricky in a new unproven situation, so The Circle Theory is one way to get everyone to understand the rules. It's simple and straightforward, but it does require, in the beginning, some monitoring, particularly where there are new people whose reputations have not been established.

While you really have to delegate, you are still the final accountable person. You cannot abrogate that responsibility. Setting up automatic reporting systems helps you to monitor without interfering, and setting them up to mange by exception is the best way of all. If you don't know how to do that, as mentioned previously, learn. It's a great management tool.

Measure, Measure, Measure

Of all my friends, the smartest was my tailor, for he constantly measured me anew, whilst all the rest judged me by my former measurements

One night I was having dinner with a friend who ran a successful middle-market investment fund. We were on a trip to see a company where the investors were fed up with the CEO. He wanted me to consider taking that position. The conversation drifted towards a discussion of management qualities we felt were important to evaluate when one spends time at a company deciding whether the management knows what the hell they are doing.

I asked him what he thought was probably the most important quality in a management team.

He didn't even hesitate. "I ask them to tell me how they keep track and measure what they do. I want to know in all areas; Sales, do they track daily, weekly, and against a target. Cash flow, accounts receivable ageing, inventory-to-sales ratio, project deadlines, production scrap rates, and product returns. Does everyone concerned know and review the measurements, not just top management?"

We shared the fact that this was basic stuff for large mature companies. Then we compared the many smaller companies we had had contact with who simply did not practice many of these basic management functions.

We agreed that it was risky indeed to consider an investment in a management team that did not routinely measure themselves and their people against pre-determined benchmarks or targets.

A side story on benchmarking.

When I was in mainframe sales at IBM, fresh out of college, with no business experience—except summer jobs like deckhand on a marine research vessel out of Woods Hole, train baggage loader, highway construction flagger, and shipyard rigger; it was a whole new world for me to suddenly be held accountable in a real-world, career-path job.

IBM was an incredibly well-managed company in those go-go days and they couldn't have been so successful if they had not believed and practiced "accountability." To really practice it, you have to have measurement standards, and, aye, that they did.

For instance, every week at our branch sales meeting, each of us had to stand and report our progress on closing accounts we had forecast 30 and 60 days earlier. It could be embarrassing, when every week in front of all one's peers, a tough and no-nonsense sales manager asked you to stand and tell about your results against your forecast.

IBM was measuring every week, everywhere, and you were part of the process. You learned to perform against the goals you had, or else, because banishment from sales was a sure path to the landscaping department.

It is quite simple for a potential investor of yours to check out your company's dedication to measuring. And whether it's sales, asset controls, production, or project development, be sure; not so much for the potential investor or lender, but for you and your people and the success of your company, that you are setting standards for performance and consistently measuring to those standards.

In its own subtle way sports has always been about measurement. The home run record of 60 in one season was such a target for so long for baseball players. We measure by consecutive games won without a loss in all team sports.

Look at golf. It's your handicap, and if it's over 18, you mumble it. You get the point.

You must have measurements institutionalized in your business.

I can think of few endeavors where a person gets a report card every single month as the person running a business does. You are measured on sales and profits monthly, quarterly, yearly, year in and year out. There is unrelenting measurement.

If you do not have a built in reporting system to give you the real reports and the exception reports on a daily, weekly, and monthly basis, set it up now. It's not difficult.

It's important, of course, to decide what reports you want, but there should be no more than five to seven that will give the important pulse of the company. Professional managers usually "manage by exception." This basically means you set it up so that the management reports you get are only those where something is off budget or target by, say three percent or more.

The difficult part is taking the time to read them, and then setting up action plans if the numbers aren't happening in some area.

But that's another discipline.

First you have to know.

Start by measuring!

Bottom Up Bias

People who think they know it all are especially
annoying to those of us who do

Too many Chairmen and CEOs develop a narcissistic arrogance about their positions. Their assumed knowledge leads them to lose touch with reality.

A few successes sow seeds of ego that spawn a conceit of omnipotence that rages through their personas.

Beware the lowly vassals who dare to challenge their liege with facts about market place realities, or any other realities!

Without question, one of the most prevalent and pervasive problems I have seen in private companies where there is little corporate governance is that the founder or non- executive Chairman is imbued with an overwhelming sense of superior knowledge and a concomitant false sense of what the customers really want.

Normally a person in such a position fills a necessary corporate function. However, he should not move out of his comfort zone to proceed audaciously into an area where he's out of touch.

No one knows the market and the customers better than the people at the bottom who deal every day with the realities of the market place. There should be a regular forum for these people to express their thoughts and ideas that generate from the source that feeds the company.

There are the rare geniuses, and bless them, for they multiply inspiration beyond what they themselves ever intended. From the legends of Henry Ford, Thomas Edison, Rockefeller, Carnegie, Mellon, Bell, and Sloan to the modern brilliance of Walton, Gates, Dell, Welch, and Buffet, we draw knowledge and respect for their visions.

To a person, they had a rare, innate understanding of what people wanted and never lost focus on delivering to a mandate they heard, listened to, and understood.

I saw many manifestations of bottom up practices at the two extremely well run large public companies I worked for; Time, Inc., and IBM

After that, on my chosen path of entrepreneurship, I tried, sometimes successfully and sometimes not, to incorporate bottom up practices at my own start up. My company grew to $48 million over the years as a result, I do believe, of offering what customers wanted, at least most of the time.

Let me recount a bottom-up example that happened early in my business career. I have never forgotten it.

It started during the 30-day boot-camp-like sales training session IBM had all its mainframe sales people go through in Endicott, N.Y. There were back-to-back 30-day classes month after month as IBM raced to keep up with and maintain its dominant position in the market. I was in a large class, and for some unknown reason, was elected president of the class.

That's only important to this story in that IBM always sent one of its top executives from New York City to Endicott to meet the class and give an inspirational talk at the graduation ceremony. The senior executive always sat next to the class president, who also had to give a short talk.

Gil Jones visited as our class's guest executive. He headed sales for IBM. He was Number Two at the company, and we were all nervous as hell, but it went well.

About three months later, I was at a computer convention as one of the IBM sales people giving demonstrations of some of IBM's latest equipment.

I had just finished one of those group demos, and from the raised platform I was standing on, I saw a bunch of blue suits who had been watching. I saw my branch manager, three other branch managers, two regional managers and one divisional manager all gathered around "himself", Gil Jones.

I thought maybe they were all practicing for an invasion of some poor third world Republic.

Every one of the managers wanted a piece of Jones's time since he had flown in from New York for just 8 hours.

Here it comes!

Gil Jones yells up, "Hey, Lee Pryor," grabs my hand to shake and says, "Can you meet me upstairs in the coffee shop for lunch; I'd like to hear what's really going on in the field."

Talk about reaching from the top down to the bottom!

Not only did I meet Jones for lunch, but he kept asking questions. You know what, he listened and took notes.

What did my customers think of the newly announced computers? How were they accepting the long delivery schedules? Did they like the SE (systems engineering) support and was it really worthwhile? Who were my toughest competitors and why? How was the new commission plan for sales people working out; was it fair?

Needless to say, when I got back to my branch office the next day, my manager, who had witnessed my epiphany, was quick to discuss enlarging my territory and was even inspired to inquire whether I might need an increased base salary.

Hopefully Gil Jones went back to New York with some real skinny, not just information filtered to fit what others thought he wanted to hear.

But for me it was an incredibly useful lesson to learn early on in my business career.

I was brought up in a military family where my father spent his career.

What Gil Jones did that day violated every known cultural mandate of the military bureaucracy.

I had been so brainwashed growing up as a military brat, that I almost thought it was illegal for Gil Jones to invite me for lunch without going through my branch manager.

Think of it; I thought the number two person in IBM might be committing a federal offense by defying the only culture I had ever witnessed, the Navy's hierarchal system.

I told you I fell off the turnip truck twice!

The bottom-up culture was ingrained in IBM's philosophy. Management understood its importance and did not resent it. Almost all great companies practice it today.

IBM in those days practiced listening to its customers and its sales force all the time, not just lip service, but real listening.

These days it's even easier to listen to customers, but so many companies don't that it's frightening.

I once ran a company that hosted thousands of Web sites for its customers. We had a simple, cost-free polling and quiz module embedded in all their web sites. We kept telling our customers that they could use it at any time to ask their customers questions or poll them on ideas.

Not one half of one percent of those sites opted to use this module, and yet you can bet that they all swore they were listening to their customers. If you are not going to listen because you know all the answers, then don't say that you are listening.

If you are going to listen, then institutionalize it like your accounting and sales reports. If you want the truly unfiltered truth you will have to establish a bottoms-up system that works. For you and for your customers.

Focus on the Core

Management that forces a consistent focus on the core business almost always develops a winning business.

I've seen too many entrepreneurs including myself, wanting to try something "new" or "exciting," when the same energy focused on the core business would have brought better results.

Much of this non-focused approach comes in the DNA of many entrepreneurs. Restless, curious, short attention span, high energy, and constant new challenge are all traits of many creative souls. But once you are embarked on a course you have got to focus relentlessly on making that course a success.

As an aside, I think successful scientists, musicians, authors, artists, and athletes are a great example of focus and discipline. There were hundreds of talented artists painting during the impressionist period in France. How many Monets were there? You can name the successful artists of that time on one hand. Thousands of artists of the period had great talent and there was wonderful intent, but less than one percent actually were successful. What distinguished them, besides their incredible talent, was their focus and their discipline.

They did it instead of talking about it.

How many people say, "I should write a book," or "I have a great idea for a company?" How many actually carry through?

Focus!

While my experience is rife with examples of executives who for the life of themselves could not stay focused, one of the glaring examples follows.

The company was in the diskette duplication business. One of its biggest customers was Microsoft, who, while they duplicated their own disks, couldn't keep up with the demand. So this company handled some of Microsoft's overflow.

The company also had several other fine smaller emerging software company customers who believed in contracting out disk duplication. Software development was their core business, not duplicating disks.

This troubled disk-duplication company had many of the attributes of a "nag" business (more about this in the brief strategy section later). The cost of entry was low for any entrepreneur with a few thousand dollars. It was price sensitive since there were a number of such companies around, because--- you've got it--- the cost of entry was so low.

Also there was nothing proprietary about it. In addition, it was labor intensive and had low gross margins.

So it seemed to the founder/CEO that the way around this was to acknowledge these generic qualities and get into some other business. Maybe not a bad idea, but the concept of focusing on the core business seemed to escape him.

In any case, too much time was being spent looking at other opportunities rather than focusing on the business the company was in.

Things were beginning to go to pot! Production errors were increasing, delivery times were being missed, and quality problems were too frequent.

Meanwhile there was a fast growing demand for software and any sub contract disk duplicator who could stay focused on furnishing a quality product on time would be able to do quite well.

But the CEO felt there had to be a better answer to his profit problems and that the answer did not lie in a renewed focus on disk duplication.

After a brief struggle to stem the downward spiral of the company, it became clear that a prolonged lack of focus had wounded the company to the point where a merger or sale was the best solution. The company merged into another one which merged into another until everyone was taken out of their pain.

I wish there were a magic way to force leaders to focus as well as to see things the way they are. The good ones do, and the not so good ones need to learn how to.

So it's up to you.

You could have that accountant trailing behind you everywhere you go saying: "Focus, Focus. See it the way it is; See it the way it is!"

That accountant is getting busier and busier! Just don't let him run the business. At least not yet!

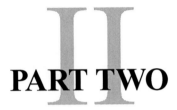

PART TWO

THE PEOPLE CULTURE

Just as companies develop a recognizable culture, so do managers in the company develop cultural habits and traits that distinguish them as effective and accomplished individuals.

Listen to the Bad News

This subject is critical. Most people rebel at hearing bad news. It's certainly not in an entrepreneur's DNA.

Unfortunately, however, a lot of what you do as an entrepreneur is to help solve problems. That's one of your primary duties. It's one of the things you're paid for.

Solving bad news makes for good news.

It means you have to not be afraid of bad news.

I often tell my managers that running a business and complaining about bad news is sort of like being a cab driver and complaining about traffic. Bad traffic comes with the territory for taxi drivers, and if they complain about it all the time they sure as hell are in the wrong business. If you complain about hearing a lot of bad news, you should be doing something else.

Or doing something about it.

If you develop a culture with your people that you are the type who can't bear to hear bad news, you're going to get blindsided someday with something you could have done something about.

I once had a chairman who was so afraid of bad news that he would often say on my calls to him, "only tell me the good news, I don't want to hear bad news."

Because of my proclivity towards running mostly troubled companies, I usually came in as CEO, but in many cases I had a chairman I worked with.

Many times he was the largest shareholder who for some reason didn't know his tea kettle about running a business; or if he did, I guess I wouldn't have been there.

I have managed all kinds of businesses for these teakettle types, none of whom wanted to hear bad news.

The prevalent pedigree of these types are the son of the founder, son-in-law of the founder, rich kid with more money than brains, and lucky entrepreneurs who believed their own press clippings about their initial success.

I really can't say which kind is worse. I also know there are many competent ones out there in that mix, I just haven't worked with them.

But if you forced me on the issue of who is worse, I would have to say the rich kid with no brains. I have stories on all of the above types and their total aversion to hearing bad stuff, but the most revolting and most blatant example of horrible mismanagement I have experienced was a rich kid chairman with a full bank account and an IQ below the par of an average golf course.

This particular guy violated every known expert business practice ever invented. It was so flagrant; I began to think he was doing it on purpose as a secret training primer for executive bad practices, and I just was not aware of the training program.

This executive not only displayed the quality of not wanting to listen to bad news, he also had a built-in sensor that would never allow him to see things the way they were. I'm not sure these two deficiencies always come hand in hand, but I feel I see an undeniable correlation.

Somewhat like the Plant Watering Lady story, I didn't think all that much about it when I witnessed the first case. But when I came across three chairmen in a row who wouldn't listen to bad news and who wouldn't see things they way they were, I thought maybe it was time to retreat to Puerto Escondido, live on the beach, eat coconuts and watch sunsets.

As an amateur student of history, I am often struck by the successes and failures which are determined by military leaders and their approaches to just these two qualities; willingness to listen to bad news and seeing things the way they are.

Two short examples.

Hermann Goering, the German Air Minister for the Luftwaffe in WWII, would not listen to the bad news of how his state of the art Messerschmitt 109 fighters were being decimated by Britain's Spitfire's over England during the Battle of Britain. When the Brits just kept coming, the German invasion of England had to be canceled just a few days before it was to start.

Hitler decided that Germany would not invade England unless Germany controlled the air space. Until three days before the beginning of Sea Lion, code name for the invasion of England, Hitler had been led to believe by Goering that Germany controlled the air.

What went wrong? Goering wouldn't see it the way it was or listen to the bad news. Hitler, for too long, made the assumption Goering was telling him the truth about German air superiority. In addition when Hitler found he was being misled he would not deal with the incompetency of his Air Marshall.

While this case is an excellent example of classic miss-management, if it had been managed properly we'd probably all be speaking German.

On the other hand, Alexander the Great listened to the bad news about the incredible strength of Arab forces massed in front of him in the battle of Issus in 333 BC.

After taking a few deep breathes, Alexander executed a night plan for his much smaller Army to go around the Arabs and come in from behind. There the Arabs were, caught in their tents smoking hookahs, and it was all over. The Arabs assumed Alexander only did daylight frontal assaults. Alexander had listened to the bad news and adjusted.

So listen, absorb, and act.

Turn bad news into good and conquer your world!

Close the Loop

Closing the loop could also be called following up, a practice that is woefully lacking in much of corporate America.

I have heard from consultants, and large corporate types that not following up on action plans and closing the loop is one of the biggest shortcomings large businesses have.

I know from my entrepreneurial experiences that the lack of closing the loop is also a huge problem in small and middle-size emerging companies.

So let's address the loop.

You have a meeting where you decide to take some specific action to solve a problem or take advantage of an opportunity.

You have opened the first quarter of the loop.

Then a lot of energy and brain power at the meeting goes into establishing the best possible solution or action plan.

You now have half a loop.

Creating the first half of the loop is fun and challenging. It proceeds quickly.

But many steps in progression have to be taken to close the loop. These are laborious and time consuming. It's where the real work is.

It's why so many loops aren't closed.

People seem to love to identify problems or opportunities. They can talk about them for hours. But when the next day comes and there needs to be relentless, unending follow up, many seem to lose interest.

Closing the loop is management and people intensive. It requires organization and discipline. Some loops take two weeks to successfully close. Others may take a year or longer.

I always felt there were two kinds of loops.

One is the one-time project, like installing a CRM (customer relationship) package that needs to be interfaced with billing and accounting software. Once it's installed, and debugged, that project is over. The loop is closed.

The other kind of loop, for example, is a customer retention and enhancement project. A good example might be an upgrade-the-order project. The loop is opened when it's decided that there should be an attempt to upgrade all orders. The profit implications of a larger order size for the same transaction are more than considerable.

This is not like upgrading a software system. This sort of loop needs to be constantly and forever monitored.

It's training, management, and monitoring intensive. It's a loop that closes, but then must be watched constantly to see that it remains closed.

You as an entrepreneur or manager must use all the crutches that are available to keep things on track and monitor to be sure the loops are closed and stay closed. Projects must not be just envisioned, they also must be completed.

Every successful manager has their own way of tracking. Use the software packages that are available or use your notebook follow-up system. Just use something.

Don't count on your memory. You may have an IQ twice your body weight, but I can tell you, you ain't going to remember everything.

So have a system and insist that every single loop opened is a loop closed!

Respect the Bean Counters

There are a lot of places a badly run company can get in trouble, but not getting the numbers on time and accurately is right at the top of the list.

Conversely a well-run company always, well almost always, has accurate numbers on time.

Let's assume that your angel investors, your venture capitalists, and your bank have approved your strategy story and accepted your capability to manage the business. Or a second stage investor believes in your company's possibilities and decides to invest. You now have the money you need to go ahead.

The next concern on their part is to be sure that the numbers they get from you are correct and on time. Part of the reason they want timely numbers is to know what is going on with their money. Another part of the reason they want the numbers is to be sure you know what is going on.

Therefore it is imperative that you have a competent accounting/financial type.

And, whether, depending on your size, they are a chief accountant, controller, treasurer, VP finance or CFO, pay attention to them, help them when he or she needs help, and listen when they bring bad news.

Remember the bean counters are the messengers, not the causers.

Together you can analyze the facts. Once identified, you can the meet with the causers, and come up with a solution.

Maybe it's an executive who is the problem, maybe it's the competition, maybe it's the strategy, maybe it's the product, maybe it's pricing, or maybe it's all of the above. In any case the bean counters give you the information you need to know to identify the problem. So don't intimidate them. Make them feel welcome and encourage forthrightness on their part.

They will furnish a great deal of your good news; and your bad news. Listen to both.

My experience has been that one of the most glaring areas of neglect on the part of entrepreneurs when it comes to managing the company, after people management, is asset management. Cash is always precious and managing the assets effectively is one of the best places to find cash.

Conversely, managing assets ineffectively is one of the travesties of entrepreneurship.

This is another place where your bean counter plays an important role.

Accounts receivable and inventory mismanagement alone have broken many a start-up and mid-size growth company. The top execs are concentrating on marketing and the "essence"(whether that's the service or the product) and have to force themselves to listen to the bean counter telling them things are getting out of hand.

Asset management is so important that I have it in another section as its own separate subject.

Let me close with a story about working with accounting types, affectionately called bean counters, that it took me a long time to learn.

At the computer supply company I started, I found that I spent the first two to three years primarily working on sales and marketing. That's what I knew best, and that's what was making the company grow rapidly.

I finally found a good production/operations guy and so, fortunately I didn't need to spend much time with the "essence," –the products. We sold (B to B), business to business, so we had to bill the customers with 30-day payment terms. That was industry practice. It is also tough on cash flow.

By the second year, we had to bring the accounting in house since it had become too expensive to outsource, and I wanted better control.

By the third year, I noticed that the monthly P& Ls were coming out later and later each month.

It was like getting fat slowly.

The target had been 10 days after the end of the month Then when I turned around it was 12, then 14, and then one day the P&L came out 18 days after the end of the month.

I was concerned because the gross margin numbers had been slowly going down. Not a good sign.

Then one day I read in the business section of the paper that a well-known publicly held company had announced that its previous month's earnings indicated that it was on track to make the forecast annual earnings.

I happened to look at the date of the paper and it was the 11th of the month.

It hit me! If a billion dollar company knows its monthly results by the 10th of the following month, you mean my little, at that time, $9 million business had to wait until the 18th?

Now I know you accountant types are wondering where I was when they passed out the beans, but don't forget about the turnip truck and the political science degree I had from Northwestern.

I was learning on the fly. That's one of the reasons why I wrote this book in the hope of helping others by-pass as many mistakes as possible.

The-one-one lunch with my controller in my office for the next day was set up immediately.

Turned out that my bean-counter felt that to give me accurate numbers, he had to wait to get bank reconciliation finished and be sure all the freight bills were in from the previous month. He said that none of it was available until after mid month every month. That's why the statements couldn't come out until the 18th of the next month.

That's when we had a little heart to heart.

Turned out the bank statement always reconciled and the freight bills were predictable. He needed to be reminded by me that we were not a public company. As such I wanted him to add a reserve for a bank error and also for any late freight bills. He could make adjustments at the end of each quarter. I wanted the previous months P&L by the 7th of the next month. Every month!

So that the god of Generally Accepted Accounting Principles, better known to the trade as GAAP, would not strike him dead each month I agreed to call it a "flash" report.

You know what, the flash report on the 7th of every month and the real report on the 18th hardly ever varied.

It's difficult to rank who are your most important key people, but don't relegate the accounting financial position to the second level. It is as critical as the others and in many cases it is the most important management position you need to fill.

Nobody said all this successful entrepreneurial business would be easy!

Be Clean, Stay Clean

It seems that about every decade or so an entire cadre of arrogant CEOs surface with the feeling that they can bilk their investors and employees. They evidently feel they have been anointed to be above reproach, so they begin to take advantage of their self-anointment.

First, it's their expense accounts, then it's charging their city dwelling to the company, then it's the art they purchase, then it's the trips. They make a science out of taking advantage of every undefined thin line between company and personal expenses.

If there can be any doubt in anybody's mind, so goes their credo, charge it to the business and justify it later. The Boeskys and Milkens of the '80s were an egregious example of bending rules and laws. They went to jail, and it calmed down for a while. Then in 2002 it started again with Enron, Tyco, MCI, and others. It's as if there is no corporate governance memory. Or they just don't care, and really believe they can get away with it.

It's the arrogance of power, and it happens to apparently perfectly fine people, because power seems addictive. Sometimes it seems that unrestrained power is worse than drugs.

As a small, growing-company entrepreneur there are not nearly as many temptations, because you are working so hard to make that initial success. It seems that it's after one has got it made that one begins to get carried away with the power. We all know the saying that absolute power corrupts.

I had a case where the entrepreneur didn't even have it made yet, but he just had to play around with other people's money entrusted to him.

I had come in at the bequest of the majority investor group as an interim CEO of this small publishing company.

In this case it was quite simple. His Board of Directors pal; a guy he had appointed to the Board, asked him for a corporate loan so that he could buy a second home condo at a resort golf course where they both were members.

It's a long story how I found out about it. The loan wasn't on the balance sheet and there were no loan agreement papers. It wasn't the first time an accounting clerk, working late, felt comfortable enough and trusting enough to bring an irregularity to my attention. Nor has it been the last time.

There it was under payables. No interest charge of course. Nada, zip, zero recording of the transaction as it was supposed to be booked. A CPA performing a random audit check could have easily missed it. Meanwhile the company was missing its bank debt reduction obligations.

Need I say more? It just wasn't worth it for the entrepreneur to "loan" his director friend money that was not his.

Be at peace with yourself and early on draw some mental line that is rigid, that you know is right. Test against it when you are tempted by the thin line of what may be right and what may be wrong.

In fact if it's a thin line forget about it!

If you are wavering, think about your board, your investors, and your employees. Think about the whistleblowers who will appear. It's better to lose it all and walk a beach than it is to be locked up.

Some people need the threat of punishment, but you should do what is right because it is right! Be clean; stay clean.

Activity Does Not Action Make

Good judgment is the child of taking the time to think
through all the future ramifications of a present decision

Not too long ago one of the most respected investors in the nation made the following observation: "If only more CEOs would stop what they're doing from time to time and just sit or walk around in their office and take the time to reflect and contemplate, we would see many more successful businesses."

We all live too much in a falsely urgent present. E-mail, the phone, and meetings drive daily activities so hard that there is little time for reflection and intellectual analysis.

Stop from time to time.

Turn off e-mail and the phone. If you feel guilty, close the door in case you think someone may walk by and think you've gone loco noco because you're staring at the walls. Then take a few deep breaths and "take 10." Start thinking about something other than what's on your PC screen. You will be rewarded; so do it!

When I was running a company in Seattle there was, of course, a lot of local lore about Bill Gates. One story, which I believe to be true, was that he would go alone into the mountains for a week or so every year and stay in his cabin and think. What a great refresher; and even if not quite accurate; it makes the point that activity does not action make.

Sometimes it's beneficial to change locations within your office when you want to think. You probably do most of your work at your desk where the PC and phone are.

When you want to think something through, put the phone on mute, turn off instant messaging and turn off the e-mail bleeper, I hate those things, so mine is always off, take a yellow pad and sit down in a chair.

Even if you take only 20 minutes, think through and even sketch through a problem, opportunity, or decision you have on your mind.

If you have a complex problem or challenge, sometimes it's wise to consult with a board member you respect. If you don't have a board of directors, consult with an experienced business friend. Getting second thoughts on an important decision is almost as important as getting a second opinion from a doctor on an important medical issue.

With good advice and thoughtful reflection you can make a wise decision. Slow down from time to time. Think!

Communicate

My Swedish friend loved his wife so much, he almost told her

No matter how you look at it, life is communicating. The better you do it the better off you're going to be. Porpoises, birds, and apes communicate constantly; much more than the average human.

So what happened to us?

That could be a long story. But I can tell you my experience has shown that lack of communicating effectively is another one of the biggest failing many entrepreneurs have. There are so many constituencies you need to deal with that it does become a challenge.

Let's look at a few.

Customers:

Depending on whether you have a few large ones or many small ones, you have to set an almost daily discipline to be sure you or some of your people are constantly in touch with customers. When things are going well, it seems there is no need to. But you'll find that problems that do come up will be solved much faster if you have been in regular contact with that customer.

Employees:

Everyone always talks about how important it is to be constantly in touch with your own people; and they are correct. Just as you systematize your reporting and project schedules, you should do the same in your communication with employees.

Any important event or happening is a perfect time to send an e-mail to your people. These kinds of things happen all the time. You have to remember that they would like to hear, so take the five minutes it takes to tell them.

Investors:

This is where most entrepreneurs are the worst; and when you start to miss the numbers; which most entrepreneurs do at one time or another; that's the time when you need them the most.

If you have been in touch on a regular basis, it will be infinitely easier to get through the rough times, like when you desperately need a little more working capital.

Send good news often, but not too often. Don't exaggerate. Send warning signals if you are going to have bad news. Investors hate to be blindsided with bad news after hearing a ton of good news.

Suppliers:

Most entrepreneurs overlook this one, but suppliers can be extremely helpful. First of all, if you can't get that money you have just run out of, you will find that suppliers who trust you and like you will wait a month or so longer than normal to be paid. If you've been ignoring their calls and not understanding their problems, you will get no help from them.

Another hidden advantage of a really good relationship with a supplier is the amount of information you can get about your industry. Not secrets, just general movements that can be helpful for you in planning.

If you need to hire someone, a supplier may know someone who is looking, plus they can give you the reputation of a person that it might take you forever to find out about.

Lastly, set up a regular communication reporting system. You certainly have a Monday morning report on last week's sales by product line to budget. But do you have communication objectives and reports?

Think about your communicating opportunities, and then just do it.

Drill Down

He always talks who never listens; he always drinks who never thinks

Have you ever noticed that when someone asks you a question, before you can barely finish a one-sentence answer, they start talking about themselves?

I've made a point of tracking this; and it rarely fails to happen.

"Hey, Lee, how was your trip to China?"

"Well, first we landed in Hong Kong and then ....."

"Oh, yeah, funny, I was in Hong Kong for awhile before going to Shanghai; I'll never forget right after landing I ......" and on and on they go talking about themselves.

What have they learned by talking about themselves? You can learn something from almost anyone by listening. If you're not learning, drill down, and you most always will learn.

It is important that when you are interviewing someone for an entry position that you drill down.

"Where did you go to school?"

"Purdue"

"Good school; what were your favorite subjects?"

"Electrical engineering."

"How were your grades?"

"Mostly A's."

"That's great. Do you remember what your class rank was when you graduated?"

That is an example of drilling down. You should ask those questions because you're interviewing for an important position. Their answers, in the worst case, tell you about their academic excellence. In the best case, you may have noticed their body language and voice patterns.

Were they giving you signals about honesty and candor? Were they looking you in the eye? What about energy, enthusiasm, and empathy? Were they crossing their arms? Body language is the subject of an entire book that you can buy if interested.

In the meantime you have taken the time to drill down enough to have learned something.

By the way (just an interview hint) never read the resume back to them as your format for asking questions. Put it down and say, "I've read your resume, but I'd like to hear it from you. It brings it alive for me."

Why do it that way? Because it gives you the opportunity to hear them communicate. Communication skills are an important part of every profile. If you do most of the talking, you lose out on learning more about one of their vital skill sets.

Drilling down is a concept and a practice that goes far beyond interviewing. Successful entrepreneurs drill down in as many places as they can. Don't take the first answer to your question as the last answer.

"How were sales last week on our quick-set voice response modem, Sarah?"

"Oh, we sold a whole lot of them."

"Good, how many?"

"I think it was around 150."

"Not bad. How was that to the quota we had for them last week?"

"We were about 90 percent of quota."

"Well, you're almost there; what is the quota for next week?"

"I'm not too sure, Jim, but I'll let you know."

You can be sure that the next time Sarah will know what next week's quota is. She should, because it doesn't happen without goals and knowing what they are.

Drilling down helps you learn for information sake, while it also tells you what someone else knows.

I knew an entrepreneur who said that she knew the answers to 50 percent of the questions she asked. When asking questions she had the dual benefit of both learning half the time and seeing if the other person knew the correct answers the other half.

Once an associate knows that's your technique, I'll bet you're getting a correct answer or an "I don't know" answer.

Drill down!

Leadership vs. Management

Leadership is about vision and inspiration; management is about action and perspiration.

Some leaders are good managers, and some managers are good leaders.

Few are competent at both.

However, you, as an entrepreneur, will have to be sufficiently skilled to be an inspiring leader and an organized effective manager. You have no choice. You have to inspire and sweat.

Large companies almost always divide the function so that a chief operating officer (COO) is charged with managing the day-to-day operations and a chief executive officer (CEO) takes care of strategy, vision and over-all leadership.

As an entrepreneur running a small growing business you have a few years to go before you break-out the responsibilities. But the time will come when, if you are to grow into a large profitable business, you will need to make a choice.

One of the most important aspects of the metamorphous of splitting one function into two, is the timing.

Too early and you create unnecessary increased cost and duplication of efforts.

Too late and you lose the edge that a full-time manager can devote to concentration on daily operations.

Too late can also rob the leadership position of the need for one person to concentrate on evolving strategies and, to address the issues of change in product life cycles, competitors, selling channels, and the many other non-operating dynamics of the business.

As mentioned in the Introduction, many of the topics in this book could become books in themselves. Management vs. leadership is one of them. I have addressed the issue here so that you will recognize the challenge when it begins to occur. I can't solve the timing dynamic as it's different in every industry and every company.

However, so that you are additionally forewarned, if you have a short product life-cycle business, you should figure you will need to morph the daily management and visionary leadership position into two separate people sooner rather than later.

Are your talents best suited for day-to-day administration, or is your strength as a leader, strategist, and visionary the highest and best use of your time?

You will need to decide. But you won't need to decide unless you take the first 18 months and focus unrelentingly on your company's day-to-day performance.

III

PART THREE

ALL DAY LONG BASICS

Know the Numbers

The peculiar thing about my freshman roommate at Johns Hopkins was that he always slept with his lacrosse stick. I hadn't played lacrosse at my high school in Connecticut, so it was new to me. Strange things these Baltimore guys did.

He had been the captain of his Baltimore high school lacrosse team. He was, as a freshman, at Hopkins, playing second string forward on the team that year which won the NCAA Lacrosse National Championship. He went on to become an All-American lacrosse player.

He told me that all the lacrosse coaches at Baltimore high schools not only made you sleep with your lacrosse stick, you also had to eat with it next to you, and take it with you on your dates to the movies, and sleep with it. In other words it had to be part of you.

It's the same with the key numbers for an entrepreneur. But you don't have to know them all, or even 50 percent. About 20 percent is all you need to sleep with.

You decide which 20 percent of the reports are the most important because some businesses are different than others. But I can tell you the numbers should not be known in a vacuum.

They should be remembered in terms of actual to a budget. We talked about it when we talked about the importance of measuring.

Sales for the week by product line to the budget for sales that week. Returns that week compared to the budget for returns. New accounts that week compared to the budget. Gross margin that week compared to the budget, and on it goes. But it is not infinite. Probably 10 to12 key numbers is it for what has to become part of you. Then you drill down when you need more.

You need to know these numbers because you are flying the plane, and you don't want it flying you. Also you need to be able to talk to the key people responsible when you see them, just so that they know you know.

Not micro managing. Just showing that you care and are aware is very important to people.

Lean and Mean

Many mature companies, like people, have developed some fat. Not that they want it, but they put up with it.

Start-ups and second-stage companies simply cannot tolerate costs that are not essential.

You may notice that one does not gain weight four pounds at a time. Its a quarter pound here and another quarter pound there. Same with many small, growing companies.

Every additional cost that does not go directly towards producing revenue should be questioned. Questioning should become habit for everyone.

When I lived in Chicago there was a classic story about cost and profit improvement that I heard and then used many times.

As you know, what oil was to Texas and technology to northern California, and Boston, meat packing was to Chicago.

It seems that there was a Board meeting early on at the Swift Company to discuss the competition. The industry was emerging and Armour and many others were cutting prices. Each wanted to take share of market from the other.

It was, as they say in the hog business, cut throat!

Since price cutting was so fierce, cost reduction and/or productivity improvement became the byword in order to try to maintain some semblance of profitability. Therefore the first subject at this board meeting was about productivity improvement.

After all of the discussions about being lean-and-mean were exhausted, one of the newer board members spoke up.

"We sell all of the well known pork products. We even sell pigs feet, pigs tails, pigs brains and tongues.

"Isn't there a way we can sell the squeal?"

Now that statement became a metaphor for me whenever there was a discussion about productivity's contribution to lean and mean.

Man, if you can get them thinking about selling the squeal, you have established a lean-and-mean profit culture of the first order.

One of the many ways to stay lean and mean is to also contain the big mamoo cost increasers, like the new corporate office, or the new plant or warehouse facility.

Another frequent violation of lean and mean is when entrepreneurs have an "invented here" syndrome, where they feel they need to develop all the companies' auxiliary functions in house.

Whether it's the accounting software, customer service software, sales tracking software, the warehouse inventory system, the web site content management system or the returns procedures—all of these functions have been invented, and you should never go through the cost and time of establishing projects to invent these procedures.

Adapt your company to proven packages and then purchase and install them.

Do not let your Information technology high priesthood talk you out of it.

Please go to the chapter on outsourcing and visit this thoroughly before embarking on these big babies in house.

There is a strange corollary I have noticed over the years that I have to pass on when discussing lean and mean.

Almost every time I have noticed a company, usually a large one, build a giant new corporate palace, subsequently they begin to have profit problems.

It happens so often that I have begun to think that it's not just this new cost, but it's also a mind-set that begins to pervade management. The nature of the palace project not only increases cost in all administration support areas, it also is a huge mental diversion for many executives from the top down.

Not to mention what those working in the field have to say about it!

When looking for an administrative office, check for nearby incubator space, or a converted warehouse, or even a sublease from a major tenant who has extra space. You will find that it sets the correct tone, holds overhead costs down, and impresses the investors and the customers.

It's not just these big things. The little things, as mentioned earlier, are also important in practicing the lean-and-mean philosophy.

As an aside let me relate something that happened to me when I was again, asked to consider running a troubled start-up. I believe this is a fine example of a way to quickly tell whether a CEO runs a lean and mean operation.

The lead venture capital investor in a troubled company and I arrived at the Dallas airport to be picked up by the CEO. When he pulled up in his Jaguar with "CEO 1" on his license plate, it sent a shiver up my spine.

I couldn't wait to see what the offices looked like. If we arrived at the office and there was a president parking place and then a plant-watering service and Herman Miller design furniture, that would tell me enough.

Sure, I would look at the facility, talk to the key people, and spend a few hours with the controller, but since we knew the company had blown through two rounds of financing while never hitting its numbers, our trip was rapidly convincing us that our concerns about the CEO had to be acted on quickly.

Remember what we discussed about non-performers? We always, yes, always wait too long.

Here are some hints so that when you need more money and the big boys come around to see what kind of business you are running and check to see if you are a lean- and-mean operator, you'll pass part of the test.

Don't pre-print FedEx or UPS mailing labels so anyone can just tear them off and send something expensively that just as easily could go in the mail.

Do not hire a plant-watering service.

Print your business cards on your own desktop printer using Microsoft desktop publisher and pre-perforated sheets from Office Depot.

Never, in the beginning, pay a graphic design artist to create a fancy logo unless you're in the graphics or communication business.

If you are a start up, get Office Depot folding tables for desks and be sure you have checked the liquidators for all of your furniture and filling needs.

Do not hire a plant watering service.

Try to have a small kitchen area with sink, fridge and microwaves so that those who want to can eat in.

If there is parking around your building, be sure the spaces closest to the front entrance are reserved for visitors, not executives.

Don't forget that you set the tone for lean-and-mean so you have to practice it until it becomes company culture.

Do not ever, ever, get a vanity license plate with CEO 1.

If you were even thinking about any luxury car, forget it until you are in high cotton.

Use taxis with dispatch services, not limos.

Rent compact cars and fly coach until you are making budgeted profits.

Eat lunch in your office regularly with a different employee.

Be lean. Stay lean, and then you can lighten up on mean!

Sales Is
Numbers Game

Many entrepreneurs don't come from a sales or marketing background. They are as uncomfortable with the sales side of business as a sales person would be writing computer code.

A systems engineer may think that "sales" is a lot of hot pitch talk.

To the contrary, the best sales people are listeners, not talkers.

But besides listening, sales is a numbers game. And once you have the correct sales strategy in place, it is strictly making the calls that bring in the business.

Low prospect call volume, low sales.

High sales call volume, high sales.

It doesn't matter what channel you use for sales. It can be catalog, e-commerce, telesales, direct mail, direct sales rep, or advertising and promotion; it's still a numbers game.

In addition you need to be prepared to spend the money to create the volume to create the sales. It will take seven calls, seven impressions, seven touches to close one sale. That can be expensive. It should be part of your sales planning. We'll discuss the "Rule of Sevens" later.

The biggest problem with under-performing sales comes from these eight factors:

Not qualifying the customer.
Low sales prospect-call volume.
Not calling on the decision maker.
Failing to ask for the order.
Not using the correct sales channel.
Poor marketing support.
Poor customer support.
Bad quality and delivery.

Another axiom on sales has to do with numbers. It's called "acquisition cost" and not understanding it is what tanks a lot of companies.

You have got to know your "cost per call."

You have to know your "revenue per call."

You have to know your "profit per call."

You have to estimate the "lifetime value" of the customer.

You can have any one of these out of whack, and you are going upstream with a broken paddle in a fast-leaking boat.

As an example: If you have a $60,000 salaried sales person with a leased car and a rich expense account, you have a high "cost per call."

If that person brings in one new customer per week, you so far, have a high "acquisition cost."

Now comes the moment of truth: "Revenue per call."

If that new customer gives you $1,000 in sales per month, your revenue per call will sink you. If they give you $10,000 per month and will repeat month after month, you have a high "profit per call."

Since every company's sales situation is different, you should run the numbers for your company. The results can be revealing!

All of this is just the beginning of explaining that sales is a numbers game. There is so much more—and as I keep saying—it's another book.

The thing to remember is that, once the strategy is proven, it is not Voodoo. It's unrelenting persistence.

Marketing is an Art Form

First let's define marketing as opposed to sales.

I've heard so much confusion about sales and marketing that I feel, without insulting those who already know the difference between them, that the commonly accepted definitions should be reviewed.

Sales, in the classic sense, is the process of selling a product or service. Marketing, in the classic sense, is the art of supporting the sale. For instance, in the monthly profit and loss statement the heading for the money coming in is usually called sales, or revenue. In any case it's certainly not headed marketing.

When you go to your automobile dealer a salesperson sells you the vehicle. All the literature and brochures and TV ads that get you to go to the dealer is the marketing.

There are crossovers. For instance direct mail, coupon ads, and e-commerce many times directly solicit sales without a salesperson being involved. In addition there are plenty of salespeople out there selling with little marketing support

In any case, depending on your business, you have numerous methods to use marketing to support the sales of your product or service.

There are big differences between B to B (business to business) and B to C (business to consumer) sales and marketing efforts.

Either way, there is an incredible amount of literature out there on how to increase your sales by improving your marketing.

In the past the sales and marketing tools were pretty much the same for a long time.

You could sell with a direct sales force that you hire (the original IBM model)

You could use sales rep firms, brokers, or dealers

You could open retail outlets

You could sell by mailing a catalog or direct mail pieces

You could sell by using outbound telemarketers

All of these sales channels were then supported with marketing

You supported the sales efforts with media advertising

You supported the sale effort with public relations and trade show attendance

You supported the sales effort with brochures and point of sales aids

While there were and are additional sales and marketing tools, these were and are the primary ones.

Then came the Internet boom, and the bust. But with the boom came new sales and marketing tools which were never before available. And boom or bust, these tools are not only still around, they are enhanced weekly with new tools and newer opportunities for creative marketing. In many cases using the Internet tools infinitely lowers the cost of customer acquisition.

Again, this is a management book and I don't want to lose focus, so, while I need to lightly brush on the sales and marketing topics, the real skinny is best covered in books specializing on these extremely important topics.(see Internet search engines for references).

In my experience, the sales and marketing subject is one where most entrepreneurs need a great deal of help, particularly if they have a technical, engineering, or professional background.

The point is to be sure that you study all of the tools and then apply what is appropriate for your company's sales and marketing success.

Manage the Assets

Oh, there are some horror stories here. Just ask any banker.

There seems to be a tremendous aversion on the part of any go-go entrepreneur to take the time to worry about the assets of the corporation. By the assets I mean what is on the balance sheet—such as cash, inventory, accounts receivable, finished goods, returns, and all those fixed assets like PC's, copiers, printers, scanners and phone systems spotted around like some kind of chicken pox and for which you owe some pesky leasing firm your right arm and left leg.

Parenthetically here, I do believe strongly that the greatest assets you have are not on the balance sheet. These assets are your people, your product or service, your customers, and your share of your market. But try to get a banker or accounting firm to let you value those on your balance sheet. Good luck.

Savvy investors will take these non-balance sheet assets into consideration, as does the public if you are publicly traded, in the form of your price-earning ratio (P/E).

Managing the balance sheet assets, however, is extremely important. It is one of the reason it's so important to hire a good controller. It's not the highest and best use of your talent to spend the time to know the details. So be sure you have the help you need be to be confident you are in control of the assets.

It can definitely sink you if it gets out of control.

The stories are legion in this area in the world of entrepreneurship.

Let me tell you a quick one.

A buy-out investment group had just purchased a company from a holding company that had decided it wanted to sell it because the company didn't fit with the holding companies core competence and focus.

I was asked to visit the corporate offices to meet and evaluate the key officers with the notion that the board might want to make it worthwhile for me to run the company, which had major offices in Atlanta, St Louis, Dallas, Los Angeles and San Francisco.

My visit indicated to me that there was substantial potential opportunity.

The CEO slot was open. The VP sales was weak and should probably go. The CFO was a CPA who had worked for Arthur Anderson. She had been put in the company by the previous owners. She should certainly be sound and dependable. The operations VP seemed solid, and clearly knew the operations of the business.

After reporting back to the new owners I agreed to go in as the interim CEO.

First, I let the VP sales go and took his position myself for a while. This had been a part of the going in plan.

What had not been a part of the go in plan was what I quite quickly discovered in the asset management area.

Right off the bat I discovered that the amount of receivables over 60 days far exceeded all known industry standards. Yellow flag. Then I discovered that there were no past due statements going out monthly. Yellow flag. Then I found that there was not nearly enough reserve for bad debt.

Next I found that the billing was going out from 20 to 25 days late. Now all of this is bad enough if you are wading in cash, but when cash is very tight, this kind of mismanagement of the working capital of the company is a huge yellow flag.

It had not been looked at during the very cavalier inspection of the company by the buyers. (due diligence).

The way I looked at it, three yellow flags is a red flag.

Red flags tell you several things. First, it is time to have a heavy duty heart-to- heart, one-on-one with the responsible person while at the same time putting the feelers out for a replacement.

The second thing it tells you is to start looking other places for the same kind of management incompetence.

So, where is the other big cash burner in asset management, you guessed it—inventory! And while I won't bore you with this any longer, inventory management in all five remote locations was a shambles.

Needless to say I started to search immediately for a new CFO.

As we have said all along, it's a people game and the discipline is only as good as the person managing it.

If you are asset intensive, be sure you have the right person in charge of accounting.

The 80/20 Rule

I won't assume you know what this is although I realize many business people do. They just don't think about it or apply it enough even though it surprisingly applies to many things in business.

One example is that 20 percent of your customers do 80 percent of your business. This can vary, but it's usually true.

That being said you can now figure it out and initiate plans to concentrate heavily on keeping and building those 20 percent that are the big producers for you. Or conversely maybe you should be figuring out how to get that 80 percent group to be larger customers.

In accounts receivable the same thing can apply. It's not everyone who is paying you late, it's probably 20 percent or less, so that's why you concentrate on those for collection.

But there is more to it than that. Who are those 20 percent late payers? Are they mostly in one industry? Maybe you shouldn't be selling to companies in that industry.

Or maybe it's a geographic area. I remember well a revealing circumstance at a company I was running where we sold product to companies all over the country. An 80/20 geography analysis we ran showed that most of our bad debt was coming from two well known eastern states that shall remain nameless.

However I will tell you that they both had New in their names and the second part of their names were York and Jersey.

Another place where 80/20 should be constantly examined is in product sales. Particularly, if you have to inventory products.

If you have large inventories in the 80 percent of your products that are the slow sellers, you have a cash problem.

You have got to have a handle on the purchasing and inventory of slow movers or it will hurt you. Conversely the fast movers have to have adequate inventory to maintain good service.

The last place I will mention is gross margin. Twenty percent of your products are going to have the highest gross margin. The recognition of this is critical. How can you push these products and how can you downplay the 80 percent that are low gross margin?

Or increase their price or lower their cost to improve the margin!

And you surely better not have 80 percent of your inventory in the 80 percent of your products that are slow movers!

You can apply the 80/20 rule to almost anything, but first you have to know it, and then next you have to use it.

Do it!

Honor the Investors

I can't begin to tell you how much I've seen the above statement violated. Of course, I went through the Internet bubble, and that's where a lot of it occurred.

There was a time then, lasting for a number of years, that every 27 year old in the technology industry thought it was his birthright to be a millionaire six times over by the time he was 30.

I was living in Seattle at the beginning of the bubble and San Francisco at the peak.

I believe that this whole millionaire birthright attitude got started when Microsoft gave each employee a number signifying when each had joined the company.

Let me first say that I think ranking was a great idea and the fact that stock options were given to the hundreds upon thousands of the early employees of Microsoft was also a good idea.

It was not Microsoft's fault that distributing such largess began to form a birthright mind-set in many young people entering the work force.

During some of that period, I was running a troubled small company near Redmond where Microsoft was, and you should have heard some of the interviews I had while desperately trying to hire good people. They could go up the street to Microsoft and have an excellent chance at being number umpty-ump and get all the stock options that came with it.

I had many interview conversations that went "Well what number will I be with you and how long before my options are worth two million." Hell, I was trying to help dig this company out of a hole, and they wanted to be millionaire's day after tomorrow. Made it kind of tough!

What happened that was even worse was the way many entrepreneurs of the time totally disregarded respect for the investor capital put into their companies.

Now it was true in some cases that the venture capitalists said, spend it, we have lots more. We want to be early in and dominate the market; all good business school thinking. But not good thinking if the consumer market wasn't ready or going to be ready before all that money ran out! "e-commerce"

I can't leave this subject without a quick 90 million dollar true story that was so outrageous you would have thought the entrepreneur was an eighth grader. And I am talking here about 90 million dollars down the tubes in a couple of years. Not an unfamiliar story to many venture capitalist of the time.

I know a lot about this because I did some due diligence for investors interested in buying the company from a bankruptcy court.

The net of the story, which is too long to tell here, is that the CEO violated every single good business practice known, including not honoring his investors. He even was overheard saying, "the deeper these investors get into this the more money they'll have to keep putting in because they can't afford this big a loss."

His total lack of respect for his investors and his customers led him to spend money on expensive marketing programs that had no chance of converting to sales dollars before the company's cash was depleted.

Expensive trade show participations, massive co-op programs, and giant giveaway offers are all things that are not only expensive; they have long lead time for revenue pay-off. These programs didn't come close to helping sales increase toward break-even.

Ninety million dollars later the company was no where near profitability, and you guessed it. The VC' money was gone. So was the company. The investors lost all their money and the employee's lost their jobs.

It did not have to happen, which is easy for me to say in retrospect.

When it became evident that the business plan and timing was flawed, the investors should have been told. The strategy should have been revised, and the money harbored while a new more realistic plan was put into effect based on what had been learned and what the prospects and customers were telling the company.

Here is a case where the CEO should have taken three days alone up in a mountain cabin. A few days of deep breathing and reflection on the status could have paid off in millions not lost.

Why? Because the problem was elegantly simple.

The strategy, devised by a Business school graduate who was too much into theory and not enough into reality, called for the company to use e-commerce to sell products to a primarily female prospect base. It was far too early into the e-commerce revolution. Woman in the primary target range were not yet on the Internet in anywhere near the numbers that the strategy called for.

In addition the website was graphic intense because all the techies and web graphic designers were on T-1 lines and generally had the high speed tools to use all the latest graphics goodies. But most prospects and customers had slow 28.8 dial up modems, and little web knowledge. You, as a user, may remember how long it could take to bring up a graphics at that time.

Do a few deep breaths and a small period of reflection tell you anything here?

Well, the Internet bubble burst, as it should have. Basically, early on like this, it was in many cases, "a cure for which there was no disease."

It was sort of like starting a passenger airline the year after the Wright brothers invented flight.

If you have raised money for basically what you discover is a flawed strategy, take your primary investor for a long walk and discuss your true feelings. These are very bright people and they will understand. In fact you would be an icon amongst them so don't worry about you job or your investment.

Honor your investors—and honor yourself.

Divide and Conquer

Not long ago I was on my way to take a train to Connecticut from Grand Central station in New York City. Tens of thousands of New Yorkers and tourist pass through this classic land-mark every day. It is one of the transportation wonders of the western world.

It is also a potential high profile terrorist target.

Upon entering, I stopped for a second at the top of a row of escalators that takes you down from street level into the rotunda ticket booth and information area. I just wanted to take it all in.

After a few moments of marveling at the re-furbished architecture, the terrorist thing crossed my mind. I wondered how they set up security for something like this. Then, I noticed, over at the side, five of New York's finest Police Officers all standing together, talking and having a high old time.

Having had some training in this area, I thought, this can't be. It must be shift change time; other wise they would be dispersed through-out the station There were no other uniformed blues anywhere to be seen.

I was ahead of schedule so I decided to watch from my perch at the mezzanine.

It was 10:15 A.M. so it probably wasn't shift change. I finally had to leave, but there they were all together talking away, with none even taking a glance around the station.

It seemed that at least one policeman should have been stationed at each entrance/exit. I am an amateur, but it was clear that the divide and conquer concept was grossly being violated.

One month later I was in New Orleans at the French Quarter jazz fest in Jackson Square. The fairly small park was jammed with people; and, I couldn't believe it; there over in a corner of the park were five cops all talking and laughing. I thought; did they bring these guys down from New York or is this an endemic thing in copdom?

I don't mean to demean the incredibly fine work most cops do; but it seems to me that they are best at quickly appearing at a crime scene rather than preventing crime to begin with. I assume they realize what a great deterrent they are by just being visible, but not always as if they are practicing for the barber-shop quartet playoffs!

My last story on cop divide and conquer non-practices also took place in New Orleans.

I was in the French Quarter when I came to a blocked off street. Then I noticed a SWAT team police van and at least 12 police cars parked on the street. To get around I needed to walk over to the next block. I couldn't get through because there were; count them, 14 more police cars. Becoming now and expert in police divide and conquer procedures; I decided to do a full count of the police cars devoted to this incident. Counted six more, for a total of 32. Plus three SWAT vans

What a great time to rip off a 7-eleven!

Anybody like me can see incidents like this and make a critical judgment that is not justified. But when you see it over and over again you realize how important divide and conquer is as a concept for success.

The New Orleans swat team effort turned up a vagrant who had locked himself into a room next to a strip joint. He was trying to knock the wall down to gain access to a little action.

Back to entrepreneurship now that you have a picture of the importance of divide and conquer. Now that you understand the principle, here are some areas where you can apply it.

If you have a major problem or opportunity, decide who should attack it. Only assign one person, unless it takes two. Only assign two, unless it takes three; and so on.

I can tell you, that if it's an exciting challenge or problem, most everyone will want in on it.

One of the areas that can become dangerously duplicitous is between the CEO and the COO.

You probably are both of these at the present time, but, if not, keep in mind that to be effective, these two positions, except for regular communication, need to be the quintessential practitioners of divide and conquer. If each spends an inordinate time duplicating or getting in the way of what is a clearly defined project, it can spell real trouble, as well as being totally inefficient.

The same temptation to do the other persons work is true in many positions; sales manager and marketing manager, product manager and marketing manager, and on and on it can go, unless you do not let it happen.

Don't waste your precious people resources that way.

Divide and conquer.

Even in less important circumstance I have seen too much of the cop syndrome with company people at company or outside of the company events.

Make it clear to your people that they should not sit together, congregate together, or talk together at conventions, meeting, diners or outings. They need to make new acquaintances, and talk to prospects and customers; not with each other. They can do that at The Lost Horse Saloon after work back home.

Divide and conquer.

PART FOUR

SEVEN
HELPFUL HINTS

Farm It Out

I realize this subject can be anathema in many respects as it implies jobs going overseas. But by farming it out, I mean outsourcing within the United States.

Small companies, no matter what business they are in, usually don't have the volume to make outsourcing offshore profitable.

At the contract manufacturing plant I ran in Massachusetts we were an out-sourcing facility for companies all around New England. It was a win-win for all.

We had sophisticated, expensive high tech equipment along with engineering and production know-how to be able to handle sub-assembly and testing for almost any client. Our customers used us because they couldn't even afford the logistics of the west coast outsourcing, much less overseas.

So outsourcing, or farming it out, does not automatically mean you jump on the next plane to Bangalore, or Shanghai, or Kuala Lampur.

You may find the perfect outsource contractor within 50 miles, if your company is in Boston, New York City, Northern Virginia., North Carolina, Chicago, Austin, Dallas, Denver, Los Angeles, Bay Area, or Seattle.

The classic outsource analysis is a tough one. A number of entrepreneurs have wrestled with it; some successfully, many unsuccessfully.

First and most important; you've got to see it the way it is. Too many executives let their ego interfere with a logical decision. It's the "not invented here syndrome" that gets in their way.

Here is an example of a successful outsourcing decision.

The company, founded by two partners from MIT, had invented a device that screens a person or an item to detect the presence of controlled substances, drugs, chemicals, and fissionable or explosive materials.

The two partners spent much time developing the software and specialized technology that made the system work flawlessly. They also designed the hardware that made it all work. They raised the money from a consortium of Boston venture capitalists and they needed to get into production as soon as possible.

Should they rent an old warehouse, buy the equipment, and set up production themselves? Or should they outsource the manufacturing and assembly to a technology contract manufacturer?

One partner was worried about security if they outsourced. On the other hand their investors were worried about the value of putting their money into bricks and mortar when a contract manufacturer could do it for much less investment.

After considerable deliberation they decided to outsource so that they could spend their limited capital on additional R& D and marketing.

They outsourced all except the final assembly stage. Then the proprietary module, the secret stuff, was inserted as the final assembly step in their secure staging warehouse where the device waited to be shipped to the next customer.

Now the reluctant partner was happy, as were their investors.

There are, of course, times when outsourcing is not the best decision. But if there are proven, reliable outsource capabilities; look hard at farming it out.

As a small-to mid-size company you should never write software or develop in-house capabilities for the following necessary functions, which are listed here with some of the well-known and proven outsource vendors.

Payroll: ADP and Paychecks

Accounting: Quicken, Great Plains, Peachtree

Fulfillment: Contract warehousing (use search engine)

Manufacturing: Contract manufacturing (use search engine)

Hiring: Local newspaper Internet job board

E-commerce: Yahoo, MSN, IBM

You probably have to get to over $40 million to outgrow these vendors. Farm it out where appropriate!

Eat an Elephant
One Bite at a Time

This concept is important in that many times, problems and opportunities seem to take on such enormous proportions that attacking them all at once seems to get nowhere. I've seen people badly intimidated when faced with a sizable problem or challenge.

You can keep perspective by dividing every large problem or challenge into its pieces and then taking on one or two bites at a time. Big companies all know this and practice it in spades. Large projects that are initiated up front always have their pieces defined with deadline dates.

You can do the same.

An example of "one bite at a time" happened years ago when some bright clerical shift manger with lots of empathy and a desire to increase productivity came up with a new idea to help all of the bored and disgruntled clerks under her supervision.

When the clerks doing data input came to work, they had a tray full of the work they were to finish by the end of the day. It was a boring, tedious job. The manager decided to put in the tray only enough work to last until the morning break, then enough until lunch, and so on.

You can imagine the difference. Productivity improved, frustration diminished, and-all-in all a better environment was created out of what was a horribly boring job.

This "eating an elephant one bite at a time" practice can be applied to many things, from the data clerks right on up to top management.

I remember well one company I went into as president where it seemed everything was screwed up. I couldn't find anything that was running properly. Accounts receivable was a mess, inventory worse, customer service non-existent, the sales call plan a shell, and the bank was making pay-me-back noises.

Somebody must have had devised this as a test for me!

Well, this was certainly a case where I had to "eat an elephant one bite at a time" or else be turned into a whirling dervish in perpetual motion.

The only way out was to quickly, with the managers, set short-term objectives with deadline dates in each discipline. The managers were pleased as they had not, in the past, been asked for their opinions.

Then we notified the bank people of our plan and asked for a breather. We would keep them apprised of our progress. They went for the plan; and each of us, when we had our bite to eat, began to make it all happen.

The secret was to break what everyone had perceived as a single problem; the bank wanted to be repaid; into the many pieces that were the real problem.

Do it one bite at a time!

Don't Bet the Ranch

There are old pilots and there are bold pilots,
but there are no old bold pilots

This is self-explanatory. But you would be amazed at the people who bet the ranch. Some make it, but most don't, so don't do it.

In a way, you bet the ranch to start and build your business. Then there come times when you see opportunities that seem incredibly attractive, a new product line, a small acquisition, a spin-off division that could grow faster.

All of these may be OK, but not, if when you run the numbers, its failure could break you.

But when you run the numbers and it looks good:

Who is going to do it?

What are you going to say to your board or investors after you've already given them the plan for the year?

How much of your time will it take, and what does that take time away from?

Where does the start-up loss money come from?

Hey, there are just too many questions and most may not have good answers.

Take a deep breath, have lunch with a director to discuss it so you feel you at least addressed the opportunity, and considered all of the questions.

If the new idea passes a valid strategy test, you can get the money, and if you know who can manage it without impacting other existing areas; fine.

Then bench mark it against what you are already doing. Would the same time, money, and management put into your present business be a wiser decision?

Why not focus on your core business so intently that you drive all of your annoying competitors into total distraction?

Get to the mountain cabin and work it out. Be sure you use all the logic you can, and leave emotion out of it. Not gut, emotion!

If it's at all questionable, punt

The train will come by again.

There is an expression in the merger and acquisition business that says, "Always be able to walk away from a deal." Don't ever even think about betting the ranch!

Opposites Don't Attract

It's tempting when you choose your bank, law firm, and accounting firm to go where you have friends, or go to the most prestigious firms in your area.

Be careful. If you are small and they are huge, you will be one of the smaller accounts at their marble palace for a long time, and you know the kind of treatment and personnel the small accounts get, no matter what they say!

If you engage a small but competent bank or the branch of a large bank, law firm, or accounting firm, you are going to be a meaningful account. You are going to get good people and excellent service.

When, not if, of course, you grow larger, you are going to most likely have to leave the accounting firm and the law firm. This is a quandary and a difficult time, but it will be part of your company's growing pains.

You will need a CPA (Certified Public Accounting) firm at least three years ahead of filing an IPO (Initial Public Offering) prospectus. The SEC (Securities Exchange Commission) requires three years of audited statements before you can file for a public offering, or large scale financing.

Yet when you first start and are small, for a while, you don't want to pay the rates the big accounting firms charge.

So, the probable accounting firm metamorphous from the initial lower cost firm, who checks the accuracy of your balance sheet and profit and loss statements, to the larger more sophisticated firm, occurs as you grow larger.

Same with your law firm and for the same reasons. You must have an SEC specialist lawyer available for an IPO or merger.

Unfortunately these growth pains could also present a problem with your controller's qualifications, skills and experience. You will need a financial person with registration and SEC experience as your CFO.

These are good problems to have, but they are difficult to manage. It's best that you know ahead of time what you may have to face as you grow out of adolescence.

It's costly to engage these highly qualified skill sets when you are small and, in fact, may never need their services.

Out growing your service firms and controller is a wrenching and terribly anxious and distasteful experience. You need to come to grips with hard uncomfortable decisions concerning people and institutions who have helped you immensely.

It could be a time when you need to lean on a board member or business friend who has been through it and can help you with the process.

Another common growth problem occurs when a company outgrows one or more of its managers.

If you see you are growing that rapidly, and you are happy with your key people, get them into some sort of quarterly two day seminar in areas where you think good training will help them grow.

You can find these programs on the Internet. They come in all flavors from sales to accounting to operations management project management and many more.

If continuing education is not cutting it, you have to think seriously about lateral transfer or replacement. You cannot have one member of a management team hold the others or the company back.

Please see the section on "Dealing with Non-Performers" It's an extremely important issue and usually difficult for entrepreneurs to deal with.

Giving up the advantages of being a small company for the advantages of becoming a large one are a two edged sword. You may choose to stay a relatively small profitable and independent company.

Nothing at all wrong with that.

But if you go for large, then you need to be prepared for the challenges associated with growth.

You've Got a Gut;
Don't Be Afraid to Use It.

Sometimes, as much as we believe that logic separates us from the animal kingdom, pure animal gut reaction may be the solution to a problem or an opportunity.

I certainly can't explain when that is, but there have been numerous times when a gut reaction was the solution. What you have to remember, however, is that just macho gut for the sake of it seldom leads to a desired out come.

Really good gut decisions come from knowledge and experience gathered over a period of time about a fairly specific area.

A technology entrepreneur with years of experience in his field may make some good gut decisions about the next product line for his business.

A baseball manager's gut decision to relieve a pitcher is the result of his years of accumulated experience in baseball, as well as his intimate knowledge of his players and his opponent's players.

Gut is generic, but good gut decisions are the product of many years of accumulated knowledge working in a chosen field.

Picking the correct person to be sales manager out of a field of many qualified sales people is a tough decision. It often comes down to a gut decision.

Henry Luce, who founded Time magazine, Life, Fortune, and then Sports Illustrated, was a quintessential entrepreneur. He came to know publishing, but each magazine was about an entirely different subject.

Publishing was the common denominator that gave him the gut to continue with Sports Illustrated when all, including his board, wanted him to shut it down when it kept losing money beyond the time frame given for it to get to break-even.

His gut said it would succeed. He stayed with Sports Illustrated. It became for a long time the most profitable publication in the Time, Inc. stable.

Hopefully you'll be around long enough in your industry to gain the knowledge to make good gut decisions when there is not enough evidence to make a good logical one.

Remember you need experience to make a good gut decision; it doesn't come in a vacuum!

The Bar Pitch

This has been called the elevator pitch, but the elevator pitch is an out-moded saying invented by New Yorkers. If you're an entrepreneur and you ride an elevator, except in SoHo, you are in the wrong building. Your rent cost is too high. You'd be jogging up the stairs anyhow if you had to go up, or down, no matter where you were. That's why it's now called the bar pitch.

Ninety per cent of all entrepreneurs will wear a tie or ride an elevator for the first time when they go on their IPO road show. They are then usually relieved to go back to their old warehouse where those 10 by 10 wooden beams smell better any way.

So; the bar pitch brings us to the 21st century.

Here it is, and next is why it's important.

You have to be able to tell someone what you do or your company does, in the time you have before they lose interest or order the next brew, which-ever comes first.

This means you have about 30 seconds.

To do this requires that you condense your mission statement, if you have one, into no more than three sentences. Best is one sentence.

Condensing what you do into one statement is important for the follow-ing reasons:

First, the statement makes you really focus on what it is that your company does. It lurks in the back of your mind. It becomes your companion. It's your lacrosse stick. You live by it. You stay focused.

Second, it allows you to answer the question directly, and succinctly, so that someone else quickly understands what you do.

My experience with the bar pitch has almost universally been that, after my pitch, the askee quickly offers to buy me another beer and changes the subject to football.

I don't know whether it's me, the business, or the wrong pub, but at least I have the pitch down!

Practice your bar pitch so that it just comes right out. No preliminaries. No equivocation, just say it!

"What do you do?"

"I run a company that makes a new product called a cell phone."

"That'll never fly; want a beer?"

The Rule of Sevens

Nobody ever said that being a successful entrepreneur would be easy.

It's not! And the Rule of Sevens proves it!

To close a new customer it will take seven meaningful calls on the decision maker. Not three, not five, but seven. Or that, at least, is the average.

Seven calls are what you should have in your head as the target before you're going to get anywhere.

You know how many people give up after just three calls; even if they make that many? I know of cases where the give up is after two calls.

To find an interested venture capital firm it will take seven tries. Minimum.

To completely mollify a very unhappy customer; you now know; seven calls.

I remember at one company where I was involved in some real clean up work, and every time we had a quick meeting to discuss another problem, one of the guys would yell out "It's the dam "Rule of Sevens" again. It's the only way we can approach this beast."

Now I didn't invent this rule of seven's. It's been around since the creation of earth, if you get what I mean.

It manifests itself in many different ways.

For instance, telephone numbers are seven numbers; if you don't count the area code. That's because Alexander Graham Bell figured (with all deference to A&T's research) that the average person could only remember seven numbers without writing them down.

Besides seven days in a week, it takes seven days to heal and then there's seven-card stud, seven come eleven, seven deadly sins, seven seas, and seven wonders of the ancient world.

Now you tell me that we don't have enough sevens mentioned here to make a rule?

I understand the real origin of the rule of sevens comes from the fact that the spin-orbital rates of the earth-moon interface are a circle of sevens. It's a pagan observation that has to do with why Zeus had nine daughters rather than seven. Now if you can understand all of this, you are a better person than Melopone.

The obviously most important thing about the rule of sevens is that things just don't come easily. It takes not only a lot of hard work, but also an expectation that it takes a lot of hard, unrelenting, focused work. Over and over again!

PART FIVE

YOUR IMPERATIVES

Hone Your BS Detector

If you don't have a built in BS detector; you need to develop one. This basic characteristic is anathema to the entrepreneur, because it requires a quotient of skepticism that doesn't come with the gene code.

You can over come this natural propensity to take people at face value.

You just have to work at it.

Here are some signals your BS detector has to learn to pick up. Some of these are covered in the interviewing section, but they apply as well to your relationship with employees, vendors, professional associates, competitors, and customers.

The person drops too many names or places.

The person repeats what is an obvious urban myth.

The person contradicts a previous statement they made.

On a drill-down question, the person obviously looses it.

The person does not answer your question right up front.

The person constantly avoids eye contact.

The person continually exaggerates.

The person is overly friendly and familiar.

Detecting the BS up front is important in that having to deal with this kind of person later will slow you down, will be high maintenance, and will cross you up somewhere down the line.

An effective executive running a fast-growing company simply does not have time to deal with insincerity, BS, and frivolous behavior. It is a time waster.

After work, at the bar practicing your bar pitch is where the fun is, not in the office.

Try to develop your detector using the above signals list or your own built in instincts.

But just don't get taken in by a person falsely claiming special knowledge or skill.

Hone your BS detector.

Delay the Bureaucracy

I hate to be a skeptic, but sure as you didn't fall off a watermelon truck, some of your management people are not going to work out.

Hopefully that won't happen, but you have to have the foresight to be prepared for a falling out. That's one reason why some basic policies need to be in writing.

Another reason is that most entrepreneurs are mavericks and particularly disdainful of overly organized bureaucratic organizations. However many of your employees don't share your entrepreneurial spirit, thank God! You wouldn't want them all running off to start businesses like yours!

Basic policies are important so that your people know basic stuff. You owe that to them. When are the holidays, what's the vacation policy, how are health benefits handled? Sick days are big, and you know many take them no matter what; so build it into your cost!

Then there is the occasional time when you have to deal with the inevitable, the non-performer!

You are not reinventing the wagon with this basic policy stuff, so go on-line or down to your office supply store and order the basic stock forms. All you need for every person hired are the following:

An acceptance letter that they sign. If you are a right-to-work state, which most are, they have the right to leave and you have the right to terminate at any time. If your state is not a right-to-work state then the policy documents are important as part of the signed employment agreement.

Rules of conduct, privacy/confidential policies, holiday schedules, benefit criteria and performance criteria are the minimum you need. Federal and state government agencies supply equal opportunity and other required documents.

The above covers almost all situations in a small company. As you grow, this area becomes more important. Compliance issues as well as many state and federal regulations will eventually force you to have a person keep up with and administer these functions. For now, don't hire somebody you don't need. Keep the bureaucracy at a minimum.

Also don't build in any benefits that require your company to administer when you can still give the benefits and not have to administer them.

For example it is not cost effective at all to offer a company health care plan to five people; or seven; or ten. When it becomes cost effective for them and you is when you reach 25 people. Before then, have everyone take out their own health care plan, and then you pay fifty percent of the premiums for them. Believe me, it will be much more cost effective for you and them. Plus you don't have to administer it.

Next! Don't issue company credit cards—ever! Have people who need to use credit cards use their own and submit an expense account for re-imbursement.

Next! Don't lease cars to anybody. You are not Hertz.

If some sales people need car re-imbursement, have them submit it in a mileage expense account every week. You pay what the IRS allows per mile and they take care of the car.

We'll go nitty-gritty here, but when it comes to bureaucracy, the devil is in the details.

If you grow to have a large number of office or production people, use vending machines in employee areas for snacks and soda, and use the profits to help defray the cost of a company summer picnic.

Office birthday-cake celebrations every time someone has a birthday are nice, but you let it get started, and everyday will be a birthday. Take each month and decide on a day. That day is birthday-cake day and everyone with a birthday that month celebrates on that day.

Now, no one can say I didn't read Charles Dickens.

Be Available

Not much should have to be said about this obvious statement. However, you have your tasks and you seem to be busier than anyone else; how can you possibly have time for all that's required of you? How can you be available?

Being available is all about time management, and everyone does it differently. There is really no one right way. One suggestion is that you allow a little time to walk around each day.

When I want to speak with someone, I mostly meet in the other person's office rather than have them come to mine. It's easier to leave. All you have to do is stand up and leave. Try to get them out of your office! Best way is to stand up!

Some managers have a person come into their office and say "you have another meeting in three minutes"; but now you are creating bureaucracy.

Another way to be available is to be sure your office is as far as possible from the entrance. I remember in one office I had, if I was to meet someone out front to go to lunch, I had to allow an extra 10 minutes to get the two minutes from my office to the front door.

At first it upset me off that I couldn't get out without hurting peoples feelings that stopped me on the way. Then I came to realize that leaving those extra minutes available allowed some time for me to spend with people who stopped me along the way. That kind of availability, the unplanned moments, turned out to be invaluable. People knew I had the time to chat for a few moments. I usually learned something and I found it much more valuable than having an office by the front door so I could race out to wherever I went.

I remember distinctly the complaints that the people had at Enron about the CEO constantly walking by them without any acknowledgement that they existed. And you know how he and they ended up!

One of the best ways I know to keep in touch with your people is to make a regular habit, at least twice, of a week having a one-on-one lunch in your office with a couple of sandwiches or salads brought in.

You probably usually eat lunch in your office, and it gets to be a bad habit to eat-in alone, or to eat with the same people every day.

The one-on-one eat lunch in policy should include not only with key people in all the disciplines but also many levels down.

People begin to expect it and are not surprised if you have a quick lunch with someone who does not report directly to you. Your VP sales may not like it that you have lunch with one of her product managers until she notices you're also having lunch with the controller's chief accountant, and the IT manager's data base administrator.

You accomplish many things with this sort of dialogue. You know what I mean if you remember reading earlier about my experiences at IBM.

First, you learn; so ask questions and listen.

Second, you are setting a culture imperative that helps to insure that there is no castle wall.

Third, your lunch partner has the opportunity to tell you anything that may be on their mind if they so desire.

You have no idea how many travesties have occurred in this world because the top person was shielded from the truth because of a bureaucratic reporting system.

This includes generals, bishops, presidents', dictators and Fortune 500 CEO's. Don't be one of them.

By the way, you must keep any revelations totally confidential and act on any information in a way that does not compromise your source. Otherwise you'll never hear the truth from anyone again.

The flip side is that you cannot, in these one-on-one meetings, express negative opinions about others. It always, no matter what you hope; it always gets back to them.

Spend some time to be available. It's good for you and everyone else.

Stop Talking and Listen

He was one who never missed an opportunity to keep quiet

Probably one of the most frequent compliments a successful person receives is; "he's an excellent listener." It is a given that you absolutely learn nothing by talking, unless it contributes to a dialog.

I have often reflected on the characteristics of my close male and female friends. One of the common denominators I find is our tendency to engage in dialog. The word, by its etymology, means two people conversing, not one.

I find I am not especially attracted to people who have to carry on a monologue. While I may learn something, after awhile with no real conversational exchange, they become boorish. Unless, of course it's one of the classic comedians, then I'll listen all night.

I had a chairman once who constantly returned my calls from his car cell phone. He would start with whatever was on his mind and then rant on and on. I knew he had to get his thoughts off his mind before he was mentally even capable of listening to what I had called him about, so I would let him rant.

When it came time for me to finally get a word in on the subject I had called about, he would quickly say he was coming to a dead zone, and we should talk later. He just did not want to listen, which wasn't all that bad, because on the rare occasions when he did listen, it would invariably turn out that he got it wrong or forgot.

And of course he learned nothing!

I believe the art of listening is probably handed to you in a genetic code pass-down. If it's not, then I do think you can acquire this important trait. If you're on the phone, stop everything else you're doing, sit up, pay attention and take notes if necessary. As mentioned in the section on multi-tasking; you can not fool the unseen person into thinking you are listening when you're not.

If you are together, it's much easier to see if the listener is really listening. Watch for eye contact. In most people eye contact is a reflection into the pool of their brain. Of course some can fool you.

Have you ever had a person stare at you so intently it almost seems as if there is a glaze in their eyes? They ain't listening. Just stop talking and see what happens.

Same with the person who is multitasking and claiming to be listening to you. If you ask, and this is a universal truth; they will always say they can do two or three things at once, which of course most people can, but it misses the point. There have been unbelievable errors made because some multi-tasking maven said they were listening and then got it wrong.

If it's important, focus and listen.

Be Consistent

This sounds like the Boy Scout manual. But nothing upsets people who work for you more than your being inconsistent and unreliable.

Unless it's breaking a promise; but that's another subject!

People who can't stand inconsistency on the part of a superior either quit, which is unusual when there is a recession, a mortgage, car payments, and college coming up, or put up with it grudgingly.

And it is amazing what an employee will put up with when they are held hostage by their circumstances. But they'll always be looking at the Sunday classifieds.

So people learn to work around an inconsistent boss. Before long the boss isn't getting the facts or is simply continually stonewalled.

That's why it is incumbent on you, the entrepreneur or manager, to follow up with what you say you will do, and be consistent.

Let me give you a true example.

This chairman of the board owned majority control of the company he had purchased with inherited money. Therefore, he had not risen to the chairman position on his merit or performance.

This can be the worst kind, but they also can be some of the best. This guy was at the bottom of the category of the worst.

I relate these traits of inconsistency to you so that they become alive and real.

Here are things you should never do!

He would not read his e-mails and then constantly phone for answers that already had been answered by e-mail.

He would not listen to his cell phone messages, and then call and ask over and over again for answers that had already been left on his cell voice mail.

He would say he would meet you at a certain time and then call on the cell and say he was stuck in traffic. Him not knowing, of course, that his assistant had just called and said he had just left his office and would be late.

He would say that he would call you back in five minutes to finish a critical conversation and then after you stay off the line for an hour, he would not call back.

He would set up a phone conference call and then when you stood by and put everything else aside; the call would never come because he forgot about the phone appointment.

He would ask for a study that would take days to generate, and once it was completed, he would tell you he wanted it a different way or, in some cases, forget why he had asked for the report.

Well, that's enough on these true circumstances. You get the picture.

Don't do these things to people!

If you do, you build alienation and separation and the whole company suffers.

You've got to be consistent. It is one of the marks of a true leader!

BE a PRO

*Lombardi time at the Green Bay Packers
always meant 15 minutes early*

It was in Boston; well, really, north of Boston right off the famous route 128; where I ran into a company that seemed to badly need a few lessons in professionalism.

It was a recent entrepreneurial management buy out (MBO) situation.

I had been approached by a headhunter representing a Boston bank to come in as an interim CEO.

Three engineers running a high-tech contract manufacturing assembly business had arranged a buyout of their division of a large conglomerate. The big conglomerate had diversified a few years earlier by buying businesses that had nothing to do with their original business. Later they decided this had been a mistake and began selling off non-core businesses. This was one of them.

The three engineers were into a Boston bank big time on their buyout loan. It certainly had sounded like a good loan to the bank; experienced proven engineers, facility in place, high quality customers, a growing market, and a willing high-quality seller.

The contract manufacturing company was in a sweet spot. Investors in the

129

Boston area who were backing MIT entrepreneurial technology start-ups didn't want their portfolio companies investing in "brick and mortar" assembly facilities.

They wanted their working capital to be used for development and marketing.

Many venture capitalists and investment firms referred their fledgling start-up companies to this contract manufacturer when products required manufacturing or assembly.

The concept was a win-win for everyone. The start-up didn't have to spend money on a building or some sophisticated technology assembly equipment like surface-mount machines for printed circuit board assembly and testing.

In fact, two production lines at this contract manufacturer could handle the needs for up to fourteen start-up companies.

Each of the start-up customers had its own dedicated cell where experienced technicians could devote themselves to the customer in that cell.

The shop people and the shop managers were real pros.

It should take a lot to screw this concept up.

Oh, but wait!

Now comes the lack of professionalism.

Each of the three engineers, who now, with the bank, owned the company, had fancy titles and very fancy embossed business cards with a custom logo from which some graphic designer had spent two weeks in Bermuda.

They also had reserved executive parking by name at the front door.

And of course each one upgraded his personal transportation vehicle type so that his neighbors would recognize his own upgrade from employee to owner.

They didn't have Hummers then, but if they had, you know the answer!

On top of all this, the three of them had an owners' beer party in the president's office every Friday at 3 P.M.

They had no discourse with the controller or even any attempt to understand what he was doing. And there was no one in sales.

I know you will find this hard to believe, but for the third time I found a controller juggling the books. He knew the owners were engineers and not professional managers, so he took advantage of their lack of accounting knowledge.

It had taken ten months to run through the bank's loan and they were out of cash. They were excellent engineers, but one of the things they'd failed to recognize was that when some of their customers reached a certain size and needed more capacity, the customer would leave amateurville and move to a maquila-dora assembly plant just over the Mexican border; or go offshore.

The company needed to have a stream of new business coming in as the fast growing ones moved out. But there was no sales department, or even anything that smelled like one.

Have you ever tried to milk a cow sitting on a one legged stool? Not a pretty sight. Funny, yes; functional, no.

Of the three legs they needed to have to be a professionally run company, they had only one. Engineering.

The sales and accounting legs were missing.

To be sure that you are running the company professionally, you must have competency, skill and expertise in all areas and disciplines.

It's a tough assignment, but with dedication to hiring right, constant training and improvement you and your people can make it happen.

Be a pro in all areas, because being a pro in only one can bring you down.

Keep it Simple

Keep it simple, or KISS, as it's called, is another classic business axiom, along with "location, location, location", and "stay close to the customer."

Everyone mouths these basics and few actually practice them. "Keep it simple" is a critical part of the company culture, and you are the one who has to constantly see to it that it's not just an empty saying.

One of the classic places managers complicate what should be very simple is commission structures for sales people.

I have a rule on this one that I have always insist upon. Here it is.

If the sales person cannot compute the commission while taking a shower or driving to the next appointment, then it's a worthless commission plan. Simple is also lots easier for the accounting department.

Keep it simple!

Another one. If the customer can not understand the pricing structure the first time around, it's worthless. Also a lot easier for their accounting department.

Keep it simple!

Another one. Web sites should be simple, clean and straight forward. Do not let perfectly well meaning graphics people convince you everything should, flash, glide, hip and hop. They sure have the tools to do it and boy do they love to use them. Look at one of the busiest sites in the world, Amazon, to see what I mean.

Keep it simple.

VI

PART SIX

MISTAKES TO NEVER MAKE

Don't Over Forecast Sales

Over-forecasting sales is so common and so egregious that most potential investors cut the revenue numbers in half for the first two years when they see a business plan.

It's extremely difficult to forecast sales by month for 24 months for a start-up company. Or even a new product line in an existing company. The big guys have it easy compared to your task.

They have focus groups, market studies, survey stats, and demographic break-downs, all buttoned up so that fingers can point all kinds of ways if the launch doesn't work out.

Piece of cake compared to an entrepreneur.

The big problem the investors see all too often is what they call the sales hockey stick. If they see this, the business plan usually goes straight to the shredder; even though they would love to believe it could come true.

A hockey stick occurs when you graph the sales and they grow slowly for a period of time then they curve dramatically up, like the metaphorical hockey stick in the horizontal position with the blade up.

The only way you can forecast convincingly is to perform the laborious task of building sales from the bottom up on a detailed excel spreadsheet. If you don't know how to use excel; learn. It is not that difficult. You can then continually play with the "what- if's" and sanity check the logic over and over again.

Keep the formulas that build the monthly sales as your investors will want to test your logic. This goes back to the numbers game we mentioned earlier; sales is the result of numbers of prospect calls, number of closes, average selling price, number of hits, number of mailers, number of customers, life-time value of customers, and on and on it goes.

The final reason you need to be reasonably accurate in sales forecasting is because to a large degree, it is going to tell you how much money you need to get to break-even.

If you're way off, you'll run out of money, and you know what that means to your mortgage.

So be conservative; and whether you are starting up or raising money for expansion, run a best case, probable case and worst case sales projection.

Then raise the money you need for the worst case.

Don't Withhold Bad News

Oh, but if I always had fair wind and following seas

Withholding bad news is one of the worst things you can do. Yet it is terribly difficult to face up to, whether you are an entrepreneur or a Fortune 500 CEO.

The aversion to releasing bad news is so prevalent that it needs discussing right up front as one of the most common executive mistakes.

First of all, people who have risen to CEO and most successful entrepreneurs have several dominate characteristics that have gotten them to where they are.

Optimism, ego, good will, competitiveness, pride, energy, inner balance, and many other characteristics that make for success are some of them.

These traits and bad news, do not go together.

So we can see why it is difficult for them to announce bad news.

One-way for you to handle this so you cushion both your ego and the recipient's expectations, is to issue an early warning.

You know when things aren't going well in one area or another where it is important enough for outside constituencies to know, so prepare an early-warning release of information.

An early-warning e-mail release to investors serves a number of purposes:

139

It lets the second guessers know that you know what is going on; that you are prudent enough to see that there could be a potential problem, and that you are smart enough to let people know so they are not blind-sided.

In addition, depending on the timing of your early warning, you may have time to correct the problem before it is a fait accompli.

It's important to realize that all of your constituencies want you to succeed, especially your bank loan officer. His or her neck is out there for you, and they have other people to report to.

Usually there is a weekly bank loan committee meeting, and if your name doesn't come up, that is a good thing! But if your loan officer all of a sudden has to suddenly bring your company up as a possible troubled loan, that is not a good thing.

Give your loan officer some early warnings as to possible trouble so that he or she can be in a position to help you, rather than you putting them in a position to look like they are uninformed.

Bank officers don't like that.

It makes them look bad.

Look bad bank loan officers don't get ahead! You will hurt them and they will remember!

The same would be true of a key director or two. They can help if they know what's happening or going to happen

Surprise really ticks them off!

Don't Create a
Self-Aggrandizing Cult

You will find, after a year or two, if your endeavor is becoming success-ful, that people will start saying good things about you and the company. It starts with employees, customers, and suppliers, then moves to your investors, bankers and accountants.

Multiply each of them by ten or so, and you have a lot of good will run-ning around out there.

Then comes a glowing press article in the local newspaper business sec-tion, then in the City Business News weekly. All of this can be helpful for your company. The more exposure the company gets the more customers and prospects take an interest.

But remember; it's the company you want people to think of; not you.!

Customers give business to the company and lots of people in the com-pany make it happen for the customer, not just you. Can you name the CEO of GM, Kellogg, Johnson and Johnson, Bank of America, Becton Dickinson, or of Home Depot or Best Buy? These are large companies. People and busi-nesses buy from companies, not from CEO's.

But you would be flabbergasted at the amount of money some CEOs of smaller companies pay public relation firms to aggrandize them. They thrive on press and constantly seek it out.

Reporters like it because they know that people like stories about people, not inanimate objects. Because of all of this, some entrepreneurs begin to believe what the press says about them.

They begin to think they are as good as the press makes them out to be. They begin to think they are infallible. This can lead to big trouble. It has led to big trouble.

IPO's have been withdrawn because the CEO couldn't keep quiet. Investors have stopped funding because CEOs have taken on an arrogancy of power that experienced people know will only lead to disaster.

Publicity is fine. It draws attention to the company, but just remember to temper it. There are lots of hard-working people who have brought you along, and they're going to be slapping their knees and rolling their eyes when they read that it's a one-man show!

Don't Stay With Unprofitable Strategies

This is a killer, and people do it all the time.

It's your strategy, and for some it's very tough to admit there is a problem when it's not working.

If you keep missing your numbers it's sort of like getting fat. It happens slowly, and then one day you say, "Oh my God I'm fat!"

Time to go on a diet. Right?

Well, continuing with a bad strategy is the same mind set. I'll wait another month. Just because we missed the numbers two months in a row doesn't mean that it's a trend yet. No need to diet yet

Where do you draw the line? This is what's called the gray area.

I say to my managers that there is black and there is white and there is gray when it comes to decision making.

Black and white are real simple. Everything is obvious. The decision is made for you.

But gray decisions are what you are paid for.

In my opinion as a private pilot, airline pilots are paid for making a severe-cross-wind landing in 500-foot visibility with one engine out while making the passengers think it was a piece of cake.

Who wants to pay them all that money to fly friendly sky's with the autopilot on while discussing the virtues of the Sox and the Yankees. We want them paid all that money to fly unfriendly skies; professionally.

In your case you are paid for making gray decisions. They are the tough landings. Black and white decisions are autopilot.

Gray decisions are extremely important and tough because the logic is not all there. The future ramifications of the present decision are not clear.

Gray decisions require a stew of gut, judgment, foresight, past knowledge and clear thinking.

If your strategy is not working, its time to turn off the phone and shut down instant messaging, meetings, and e-mail.

Get with a few of your best and brightest for a few quiet hours or days if necessary, in deeply focused discussion on the questionable strategy.

The problem is not going to disappear by kicking at it for a few minutes every day. You need to focus, measure, drill down, and see it the way it is.

Don't Let Daily Tasks Keep You From Communicating With Customers

We all know how important it is to communicate with customers.

However, this subject varies depending on who your customers are. If they are consumers that is one thing; if they are other businesses, that is an entirely different thing.

The key thing about staying in touch with them, no matter who they are, is that you have a system.

Again, too many entrepreneurs think there is some sort of voodoo attached with sales. It is, as said before, a numbers game. And so is customer communication.

You have to set up a system that reminds you of who to contact and when. Then you need to follow it just the way you follow progress on any project important to the company. There are numerous sales tracking and customer contact software packages available.

Customers like to be kept informed and up to date. There are people other than yourself within your company who can and do touch base with them, but you need to be involved.

Customer service can do it through a customer relationship management (CRM) package, technical support can do it, e-mail can do it, you can do it through polls and surveys on your web site; and sales people sure as hell better be doing it; and on and on it goes.

Banks found out a long time ago that if they could get a customer to use three products within the bank that they would keep the customer practically forever. Moving out of state would be the only reason they would lose a three-product customer.

So as soon as a checking account was opened, the bank would push for a savings account. Then there were other products such a lock box, money market account, CD account, and IRA account. If the bank kept their computers up and checking accounts in balance, it had lifetime customers.

Catalog companies long ago discovered that its most recent customer are its most likely next customer. Thus "recency-frequency" became a by-word in the industry; much like "location-location" in the real estate business.

Communicating with your customers in some way, depending on the nature of your particular business is your responsibility and mandate.

Not doing it because you haven't built it into your daily life is not an option.

Don't Go With the First of a Vendor's New Product

This can go both ways so we have to be careful not to generalize here.

You should always be looking for something that gives you an edge over your competitors, or something that is proprietary; it adds value for your customers and adds value to your company.

Having said that, there are legions of companies who have stumbled and even failed because they took on a new product or service from a vendor that just did not work.

So first, like anything else, don't bet the ranch. Make the assumption that it will fail and ask yourself how that would affect the company as a whole.

For instance, you are upgrading your accounting software because of your growth. You've outgrown Quick Books and then Great Plains, two of the best known and proven small-company accounting software packages.

However, your controller says he has a cousin and brother-in-law who can write a better upgrade than any available on the market and have it done in six months.

Don't do it; loud and clear, don't do it.

Same if a new firm comes in with an accounting package upgrade they have been working on since the millennium and ask you to be one of their beta sites.

Loud and clear, don't do it! It can screw up your entire company; it is bet the ranch stuff.

I have seen it in process. It isn't pretty!

On the other hand, through an unusual set of circumstances, I have had the opportunity to run three entirely different kinds of companies with the exact same circumstance that I am now going to describe.

Let's say you have seven identical pieces of production equipment that are producing the exact same product. And let's say your competitors have the same machines made by the same manufacturer.

Now the equipment manufacturer approaches you and says it has a new faster, cheaper, piece of equipment they would like you to try.

It's only one of seven pieces you have, so the worst case scenario doesn't mean disaster. On the other hand, if it works, it could mean a nice competitive advantage for a while.

So you go with the trial. In this case you have violated the concept of not going with the first of a vendor's new product.

But you haven't bet the ranch!

Don't Forget That Promises Made are Promises Remembered

A promise made is a debt unpaid

—*Robert Service*

Making promises and not keeping them is a common mistake, I have seen numerous times. You just cannot make a promise to someone and not follow through with it. They will remember your promise for an eon.

If you are one that wants to build popularity by making promises you are not sure you can keep; you have it all wrong. It's the opposite. If you don't follow through it builds contempt, then disrespect, then rebellion, depending on the importance of the promise.

I learned early on at IBM that if you were branch manager and had four really good candidates for a new branch; which you did since there were so many bright accomplished sales people; you could never, never go to all four individually and say, "You know, you're very qualified for that new management job in Anaheim. I want you to know I'm seriously considering you for the position. Would you be interested?"

Not even a promise! But in the eye of the beholder that statement sets an expectation, that if not met, is a promise broken.

Don't make promises on the fly. Don't make promises you haven't thought through. Don't set expectations that can be considered promises. Don't make promises because they make you feel better, and you think it will make the promisee feel better. It's not about feelings, it's about expectations.

If you make a promise it will be remembered.

Keep a promise. Or don't make one.

Don't Listen to Those Not in Touch With the Market

There are many drinkers at "The Lost Horse Saloon" who will give you better advice than an out of touch senior executive who really doesn't understand your industry.

You should, of course, listen to all advice because you never know where you may learn something of value. You just need to know how to determine what is of value and what is not.

There have been many cases of generically gifted senior leaders who have totally switched industries and performed magnificently. My following comments are about those many who are not capable, but happen for one reason or another to be in a position of higher authority.

I have, on numerous occasions, seen senior executives, including CEOs, choke on their Diet Cokes when hearing the advice of a chairman owner who comes up with a cockamamie idea that he feels should be pursued.

Usually there is an unspoken, almost underground conspiracy that keeps everyone stonewalling the idea until it dies a natural death. Chairman owners who are not aboard as a result of merit, and start to incessantly interfere, often have short attention spans. So everyone knows they can let the pronounce-ments die a natural death.

But if the idea doesn't die, then you have to stand up to it and explain that the idea just won't work, and why. If they own the company, it's a tough thing to do no matter how out spoken you feel you are.

During the Internet boom more investors and entrepreneurs should have asked end users if they wanted to use and understood the services being offered by this revolutionary new delivery system.

The advice they would have heard, if followed, would have saved billions of dollars from going down the chute.

They did not listen to those closest to the market.

Don't make that mistake!

PART SEVEN

IMPORTANT QUALITIES TO LOOK FOR IN THE PEOPLE YOU HIRE

The Three E's: Energy, Enthusiasm and Empathy

Energy, enthusiasm and empathy are universal qualities of success. You have to learn how to recognize them quickly when interviewing.

If you don't know instinctively how to recognize the three E's, then you have to actively think about them while listening to your candidate.

One comment on energy, enthusiasm and empathy. All positions need a high mark on energy, but controller for instance, may not need as high a score in enthusiasm and empathy as a sales manager.

However since we are talking about potential leaders here, all three qualities are needed for anybody to be successfully upward mobile.

Make your own mental checklist so you can review these characteristics when you've finished an interview. Also ask your other people who interview candidates to mentally note these traits so that you can all discuss them when you do the wrap-up review before making a hiring decision.

You should always go through at least three interviews before hiring anyone for a management position. Sometimes it takes that long to pick up on several of the three E's.

Always conduct each of the three interviews in a different place; one in your office, one outside for lunch, and another for a 7:30 breakfast.

By the way, there is no such thing as a good excuse for them being late to the breakfast!

Now let's briefly discuss each trait.

Energy:

You should be able to easily pick up on this one by the end of the first interview; and certainly by the second interview. People either exude energy or they don't; you have to watch for it.

Enthusiasm:

It could take until the third interview to detect this. This trait does not have to be noticed in an outwardly expressive way. Enthusiasm can be fairly internal; that's why it may take a few meetings to detect. Look for it. Notate it.

Empathy:

This characteristic can also be detected almost immediately. In some businesses it's called skin Q. It's totally subjective and can be best summed up with the feeling that you would just like to see this person again and feel you would enjoy working together.

By the way, you will need to bring your BS detector with you on all interviews, and don't forget the previously discussed "drill down" and "listen" practices.

Also don't forget that "fit" with your team is extremely important. As mentioned, your team members have to do their own one on one interviewing, and then you all compare notes.

Communication Skills

First, you need to look for the candidate's capability to express thoughts in a way that does not confuse you. If it confuses you, you can imagine how it'll come across to others.

To check this out, you'll need to wrap three questions into one; sort of like reporters do at press conferences.

"Tell me; what has been one of your biggest challenges, how did you handle it and do you feel you acted quickly enough?"

This way you are testing verbal skills, directness, intelligence and memory, all at once.

One weakness, or strength, which you can catch right away, is when the candidate does not directly answer the question. This failing is universal in people who aren't going to make it far in the long run, and it's a quality you can notice quickly.

If they hem and haw, or start the answer with a story or really anything except directly answering your question, it's a yellow flag.

Avoiding the question and not directly answering it indicates they should probably run high political office, and you should find someone else.

Another verbal skill problem is the use of lots of buzz words, acronyms, and industry jargon. Using these crutches is a sign of insecurity and also displays a lack of sensitivity.

The last communication skills clue would be to notice the candidate's grammar. Since this expresses itself in oral and written ways, I would ask them to e-mail you some thoughts about joining the company as a follow up to the first interview.

Intelligence

Intelligence is tough to pick up right off the bat.

I think intelligence and knowledge sometimes get confused.

While you may find someone knowledgeable, it doesn't automatically equate with intelligence. Some people think intelligence is remembering last month's numbers and what the numbers are in the projections for next quarter; or the name of the restaurant where they had dinner in San Francisco five years ago.

That is an excellent quality to possess; but it's called memory, and is only part of the makeup of intelligence.

I think another part of intelligence is the capability to think through a problem and come up with a solution that proves to be correct. This is tough to determine during an interview.

Let me tell you a story so that you can ask your candidate a what-would-you do question, which may help you determine cognitive intelligence.

A woman is driving along on a country road and gets a flat tire. She forgot her cell phone, and there is nothing close by but a state insane asylum, which is closed to visitors because it's Monday.

One of the inmates comes up to the fence to watch while the intrepid woman takes out the spare, jacks up the flat tire axle, unscrews the bolts, takes the flat tire off, and while sitting down to rest, kicks the lug nuts from where she had carefully put them, and down the sewer drain they go.

Completely frazzled she is at a loss as to what to do to put the spare tire on and keep it on with the bolts all down the drain.

This is the predicament you put your candidate in to see what sort of cognitive ability he has.

The asylum inmate, from behind the fence says, "Lady, why don't you take one bolt off the other three tires and use those three to put your spare on?" The woman is overwhelmed with gratitude and says, "That is brilliant, why are you in this institution?" The inmate says, "Lady, I may be crazy, but I'm not dumb."

Now you see what I mean about the difference between intelligence and memory.

However, no matter how many intelligence tests or questions you ask, you probably aren't going to know the answer to the "intelligent" question until after working a while with a person.

So you have to use the best estimate you and your peers can make to decide on this one.

It's a gray decision, but you have a gut; make the call!

Sincerity and Honesty

These qualities are obviously important for a person in a managing position, or any position, to possess.

Again they are difficult to pick up on quickly. But I suspect that if you have your BS detector on, it might make it easier to pick these qualities up during a second interview, where the candidate is now a little more relaxed.

Let me give you a real life example of using a BS detector while noticing how the little things are so important.

A friend of mine who is an engineer and CEO of a fast-growing company he founded, asked me to help him with a final interview for a vice president of sales.

This was a critical position and since sales wasn't exactly my CEO friend's field of expertise, and he had no human resources person, he was wise enough to ask for an hour's worth of assistance.

He felt there was something about the candidate that just missed the mark, but he couldn't put a handle on it. The references had turned out extremely well, but there was a shadow of a doubt.

I met with the candidate and was impressed with his energy, enthusiasm and empathy. His skin Q seemed great and his communication skills were excellent.

Then it happened.

When I asked him where he went to college, he said he had gone to West Point.

Now I know, and you know, that many colleges have nicknames. The Naval Academy is sometimes referred to as Canoe U or Sing Sing on the Severn. The most common one for the military academies is that the graduates are called "ring knockers." This is because the class ring is such a big thing at the academies. Each class, before graduating, has a Ring Dance and a Ring Queen. It's all part of a tradition they love and revere.

After graduation, the ring is worn all the time, so that those in the field know the ring knocker is the academy guy and should, by inference, get the most respect.

Or disrespect, depending on the situation and the individual.

So, back to the interview. While he is talking I look down at the candidate's hand. No ring! Unheard of in the annals of modern West Pointism!

I decided not to ask questions or listen to excuses, but after the interview I called the United States Military Academy. The records indicated no such person had attended West Point

My CEO friend and I were stunned. How and why would a person who had so many good qualities try to get away with lying about where he went to college? I could go on and on about this guy, but suffice it to say that a BS detector and practicing the art of "the little things" saved the CEO from what could have been a bad mistake.

Honesty is probably the handmaiden of sincerity so the two are included as one here. While honesty is difficult to pick up on during an interview, sincerity is a bit easier as it expresses itself openly during conversations.

Therefore, by the third interview you should have formed a solid opinion about the person's sincerity. This will also be a lead indicator about honesty.

This hiring business is tough if you are to do it correctly.

Organize it, set standards, rank the qualities, and compare them with the others who have interviewed the same person.

You can do it!

Practice these interview ideas, use your gut; be a pro; drill down; and see it the way it is!

Inner Balance

This is an important quality to look for when hiring for management positions. It's tough to recognize at first. The person has to have had good parenting, or been through some tough times and come out well. Unfortunately, you are not privy to any of it.

You can certainly ask the person if there was a good relationship with their mother, their father and their siblings. But they can so easily read the proper answer to these questions. You have to watch the candidates eyes and body movements carefully to get a clue as to how truthful the answers are. Then you're still not sure.

Let me tell you a story of the way one person developed "Inner Balance" the hard way.

I recently finished reading a book about the World War II Battle of Britain.

It was the Spitfires vs. the Messerschmitts.

They fought it out over England with the Brits trying to stave off Germany's planned invasion.

The year 1066 was the last invasion of England and the RAF pilots weren't about to let it happen again in 1940. When you live on an island and eat mutton and kidneys your memory and your history are important to you.

Churchill's famous, "Never have so many owed so much to so few" was a tribute to those British pilots who fought so well.

Well, with a little literary license, this is the story of inner balance.

A Spitfire pilot re-counts how one of his wingmen, who was extremely aggressive, almost to the point of being obnoxious, was shot down three times in a row over London by German Messerschmitts trying to protect German bombers over London.

The story goes that he parachuted the first time onto a cricket field during a match and was promptly chased off; the second time he drifted onto a soccer field and was drafted into the game; and the third time he parachuted into the front of the Pork and Pie pub where his squadron leader found him full of ale and promptly stuffed him into the next available Spitfire to get back up there again.

The story continues that after that third parachute ride down the Spitfire pilot finally developed an "inner balance" and went on to become a top ace.

Inner balance is probably one of the top qualities of a real manager. You are either born with it or some lifetime event or three, hands it to you.

You can't lead effectively without it. You feel it, and everyone else feels it. So you should be able to detect it in a person after a few interviews and discussions. Then check with your team and decide whether there's enough of it in your candidate.

These qualities outlined are important to look for. You can't always be right in your selection, but you can do the best you can with the best knowledge you have available without becoming an expert.

Remember, its good people who are going to make it happen.

You have the plan, the product, and the money—people make it happen!

VIII

PART EIGHT

GROWTH CREATES PEOPLE PROBLEMS

Now that we have discussed some techniques about hiring, let's discuss some problem types you may have inherited, or by some complete quirk, some of those you hired have begun to display suspicious symptoms of incompetence.

Once you can classify the disorder you may find it easier to deal with.

There follow here some true stories as examples, but in consideration of brevity, some will just be pointed out as qualities to watch for.

You will understand!

Getting Ready to Get Ready Freddy

Nothing will ever be attempted if all possible
objections must first be overcome

—*Samuel Johnson*

We've all seen this "getting ready to get ready" trait in many different people. Here are a few:

The corporate type who is getting ready to get ready to start his own business.

The housewife who is getting ready to get ready to write the great American novel.

The sailor who is getting ready to get ready to sail around the world.

The plump one who is getting ready to get ready to lose weight.

It doesn't matter what it is, and in most cases listed above it doesn't matter much if "getting ready to get ready" ever gets started.

It does make a difference in business and professions. A big difference. It affects others to a considerable degree. So it is a dangerous trait that must be recognized and dealt with.

Can you imagine at Boeing, GE, or Microsoft for instance, how long a project leader would last if he were always getting ready to get ready. He'd be thrown into the archive re-organization department faster than one can say microfiche.

The worst part is that many "getting readies" talk such a good game.

Their initial moves are illusory; they look good, and by the time you have them figured out, far too much time has been lost.

Worst of all their "getting ready" traits are so sanctimonious.

Like, "don't push me, you risk taker." "Are you sure we've thought this through?" "Has it been approved all the way up?" "Maybe we should research it some more!"

Don't worry about "Getting Ready to Get Ready" being right. That's what he's up to. Those guys who said "ready, fire, aim" were right on; most of the time. Best to move "Getting Ready to Get Ready's" ass into the archive department fast so you can get going.

Let me give you a real-life experience with a "getting ready" so you may be able to pick up the traits and move quickly on the problem.

I used to ski with a friend who was so into preparing his equipment that his ski time on the slope may have approached 20 percent, while the rest of us were at 90 percent; and if you like skiing; more than you like getting ready to get ready, then you can understand.

We would arrive at the top of the lift and his bindings needed adjustment, his boots needed tightening, his goggles needed to be cleared, his poles needed checking and of course his gloves needed to be tightened.

I could have been half way down the mountain before he was ready to start.

I later had the opportunity to work with Freddy and to my amazement he displayed the same characteristics at work. We would decide in a meeting on a certain course of action; set a start date and move on.

Freddy accepted his tasks with relish.

Two weeks later at the progress meeting "Getting Ready to Get Ready Freddy" was, you guessed it; getting ready!

Statements like this were made: "Did we really agree on this project," or "I thought of some new things we should reconsider before we start," or "I need to research this a little longer."

We would all look at each other in disbelief because we thought the project was two weeks well underway.

In one case "Getting Ready" was to study whether we should take advantage of a vendor's offer for us to be a "beta site" for a new piece of equipment that produced the same product we were making with the vendor's older and slower equipment. (This was mentioned earlier in the story about not betting the ranch).

If the new machine worked properly in a real production environment at our company, it could give us a competitive cost advantage in a competitive business.

"Getting Ready" wrestled with his assignment as to whether he should recommend we take on this beta-test project. Would it not cost us more in labor and scrap or rejections? Could we trust the vendor in our plant? Would the production employees rebel?

While "Getting Ready to Get Ready" was weighing all of these potential problems the vendor's people finally came to us and said they had waited long enough for our decision. They had decided to place the equipment in a competitor's plant since they needed to get ahead with the project.

In my opinion there are basically two reasons Getting Readies have a problem.

The first could easily be top managements fault by creating an environment that doesn't tolerate mistakes. That is common and is an entire subject unto itself.

In Freddy's case it had been clear we had a culture that delegated and expected the best but knew that mistakes would happen.

In his case, it turned out he really should not have been in a decision-making capacity with an action oriented company.

If you come across any of these "Getting Ready to Get Ready" types you have to deal with them. It can't wait.

Each is a non-performer in camouflage.

Assumption
Bumpkin Billy

Assumption Bumpkin Billy could be worse than Getting Ready, but I don't want to get into ranking as we have so many potential problem types.

One of the biggest ways to get into trouble is to make an assumption or take someone's advice who has made an assumption and then depend on it.

There are plenty of "what if" assumption game scenarios both in business and in the military. But I am not talking about the play-games world.

I am talking about the straight line in-the-trenches action business world where decisions are made quickly, and they must be made with all the available facts possible.

In the basket of facts, there can be no assumption apples, otherwise you can get royally screwed.

Corporations and battles have been lost because of assumptions on the part of leaders at the top.

Let me give you a few oversimplified examples.

The Japanese lost the battle of Midway, a turning point in the Pacific war, basically because they were refueling the planes from all four aircraft carriers at one time, which left few planes in the air. They had made an assumption that there were no American aircraft carriers anywhere around; that assumption will be studied for a long, long time!

During the Battle of ISSUS in 333 BC, the Arabs made an assumption that Alexander the Great would come straight at their much larger forces and they would decimate his army.

Young Alexander hadn't been dropped off an olive cart yesterday, so he sent his small army around and came in the back way at night while the Arabs were smoking their hookahs.

That was the end of that bad assumption on the part of the Arabs That assumption has been studied for a long, long time!

I would guess that all of us have come across assumption problems, either in our personal or business life.

Everything that's not a fact is an assumption. Maybe too many people have a hard time determining what a fact is. Sometimes there are questions about facts.

If it looks like it's going to rain, that's an assumption. If the barometer has fallen two points and weather radar has thundershowers three miles to the west; those are facts.

If you just lost an account because a competitor bid lower than you did when you assumed from their last bid that they would be high; that is also a fact.

When you experience someone continually bringing you assumptions, drill down on the assumption until it becomes a fact or does not.

You can help assumption bumpkins out of their misery.

They can be trained and they can learn.

Unfortunately, I doubt that there is anything you can do about the next type we're going to discuss.

Attention Disorder Danny

I swear I think if there had never been such a thing as Attention Deficit Disorder (ADD), Americans would have invented it anyway and every child by the age of 4 would be culturally imbued with it as part of a sacred rite of passage.

It doesn't matter whether it's TV, movies, or music, it all seems like a diabolical plot to train everyone to have an attention span equivalent to a rhesus monkey.

Attention Disorder Danny's, in business, as in any endeavor are a snare and a delusion. They will never be successful in the management world because focus and discipline, the opposite of attention disorder, have been proven over and over again to be hallmarks of success in managers and leaders.

Have you ever noticed how a great athlete, engineer, artist, writer, mathematician, architect, or lawyer; for a few examples, have incredible concentration ability?

In fact one of the distinct characteristics of success is unusual focus and concentration. Watch those eyes focus on the ball in any ball sport! Looks like they want to devour that ball.

It's amazing. I understand Ted Williams didn't even have a blink rate. His 1941 batting average of 406 is still a record. No attention disorder there!

173

On the other hand there are some professions where a premium is placed on what may seem like attention disorder but which is actually a skill set needed for rapid decision making.

Have you ever seen a really good auctioneer or floor trader in action? Each is a beauty to watch. But leadership and management are not what they are about.

Attention Disorder Danny can't really get anywhere in most public companies where meritocracy rules. However I have come across some outstanding cases of ADD managers in private companies where factors other than merit sometimes determine a high level position. Such as: "I had the money to buy this company pal, and you'll do it my way even if I change my mind every day."

I have a litany of true stories about Attention Disorder Danny Chairman and CEO's. Most were individuals who could charm the boots off an Eskimo in mid winter and did charm mega-moola from too many venture capitalists. They all seem to have a set of common qualities, which include charm, optimism, vision, extraordinary verbal skills and unbelievable displays of attention disorder.

Left to run amok, they can ruin a company.

Unlike the Assumption Bumpkin, who can possibly be trained, it is very problematic as to whether you can train an actual grown up, 45-year-old attention disorder case.

Send him to the commodity or futures pit and re-hire!

Big Hat; No Cattle Charlie

This seems to be a great metaphor for a number of people, none of whom you want working for you. This expression is an opposite of the oft-used "he walks his talk."

This person has a lot of "Getting ready to get ready Freddie" in him. "Big hat; no Cattle" has grandiose plans and talks about them all the time. Then when it comes time for some action and performance, Big Hat can't make it happen.

A short story!

This Big Hat was hired to bring in some sales for a web site company that badly needed advertising revenue.

Big Hat seemed to fill the bill perfectly for the sales position. He was engaging, articulate, made a wonderful first impression, and dropped a lot of high-level names of large companies who were good prospects for the company.

Management and even the board were a little concerned whether Big Hat really had any cattle, but the chairman, who was always bamboozled by charm and pedigree, insisted that Big Hat be brought on.

It was a great opportunity for Big Hat to bring in revenue right off the bat and become a hero rain-maker for the company which badly needed cash flow.

Instead Big Hat decided that the website needed improvement before he could sell ad revenue. So he, with the chairman spent the first five months talking about the improvements needed and engaging a graphics web-site specialist agency to work on a substantial site revision project. This during a period when the company was losing money and badly needed sales, which Big Hat thought, couldn't be brought in with-out spending money on a better site.

In the meantime management, convinced there could be instant ad revenue, engaged a part-time sales person working from his home at a paltry base salary and good commission. In no time this individual brought in, one after another, new Fortune 500 accounts that were more than happy to advertise on the web site the way it was.

This down-to-earth sales guy walked his talk, while Big Hat kept looking for his cattle.

High Maintenance Harry

You're a big wave, but you're not the ocean

I was once told that to have a happy relationship, among many other things, a person should stay away from getting involved with someone who displays too many high-maintenance characteristics.

Sorry if it's too late, and yes, I have many other personal hints of little value once the step has been taken. Nobody pays any attention anyway, do they, when passion and chemistry really rule the decision?

But we're talking business here, not romantic relationships, so lets move on.

We all intuitively know and have seen high-maintenance people at work. But here goes in case you need a reminder.

They are late to most appointments with horrible excuses;
They have forgotten some important item needed;
They have lost some important item needed;
They have to go back to get some important item needed;
The traffic light on their corner was broken for an hour;
Their child was falsely accused of robbing a 7-eleven;
Their third cousin once removed is sick so they have to miss time at work;
They have to be in court to testify about their rabid dog;

Their car was broken into, so they need to take it to the shop;

Coffee spilled on their keyboard so they don't have the report ready;

The ATM ate their card so they have to go to the bank;

The air conditioning is blowing directly on them and their neck is sore;

We could go on and on, but you have the picture. Any of these things can and do happen to people all the time. The problem is when the same person has it happening to him all the time.

The only place that I can think of that will put up with this kind of stuff is the US Post Office; they have an excellent retirement program and you don't, so maybe you should slip High Maintenance Harry an application!

Exaggeration Eddie

OK, this needs little explanation, but this trait needs to be dealt with. Exaggeration serves the person no purpose and certainly serves you no purpose.

It's important, I think, to differentiate between an optimistic persona and an exaggerating person.

Optimism is good, and it's strong, and it's necessary.

Exaggeration needs to be tempered, by you, as well as by your people.

The problem with exaggeration in business is that it leads others to presume expectations that may not become realities.

It's like the cry-wolf story. After several exaggerations, you begin to lose confidence in the person, and for them, that's about the worst thing that can happen.

For you, you begin to distrust even the not exaggerated statements, and this can lead to a state of confusion that's really unproductive

So, again, the one on one lunch.

No Compass Nancy

If you've ever spent time in the mountains, on a desert, or at sea, you know about Polaris, the North Star. It's a refreshing companion because it's beautiful, consistent, reliable and easy to find. It's the end of the handle of the big dipper

It always knows where it is, and because it does, you always know which way is north. Once you know north, you know all the other directions. In the southern hemisphere, the Southern Cross plays the same role. Just in case you are an Aussie or a Brazilian and are reading this book.

It's difficult to deal with a person who does not have a built-in internal compass. You never know where they stand on an issue or what they think. There is no ethic, or even an anti-ethic. You want to know what they think, not what they think you want to hear.

You want north; they're north. You want south by southwest, there they are. Control freaks love them. They abide by the thousands in large organizations. They love the military, where the ethic is "the right way, the wrong way, and the Army way."

Seldom do they rise to the top of a large organization; but if they do; watch out!

In a small company where individual initiative is so important, they can be a real hindrance because there are few manuals, little formality, and lots of free wheeling.

Without that internal compass, they can get lost in a hurry.

This trait is sometimes tough to discover for a while; but when you do, it's time for the lunch.

Embers-in-the-Belly Kelley

While this trait is easily detectable, it should have been picked up during the hiring interview. However the trait can develop over a period of time.

You can see Embers-in-the-Belly sauntering at a slow pace down the hallway; usually with a cup of coffee in one hand and a friendly wave over the cubicle partitions with the other hand as they stop to ask how the week-end was.

Hey, you set the culture, and this is not the one you want. It has to be nipped fast.

You need to ask ole-step-and-shuffle Embers-in-the-Belly, into lunch immediately and have that discussion about the day he was hired and you discussed how important a sense of urgency is and how he certainly agreed. This is of course when you ask if he feels he still has that sense of urgency. He knows what you're talking about.

Another story.

I dislike bringing IBM up so often, but, after all it was about my only large company experience so I will mention a negative occurrence that to me exemplifies Embers-in-the-Belly while re-enforcing other points made in this book.

I had left IBM and had totally lost touch. But one day I learned that they had an investment division that made investments in private entrepreneurial technology companies.

The person running the group was located at the Headquarters in Armonk, NY, so I finally, after seven calls, got an appointment.

Now keep in mind that my image of IBM had been from my go-go days when nobody would be seen walking. You moved into a trot when you moved. You were a man on a mission.

I arrived in Armonk at the appointed time and was waiting in the lobby, when, no, not a plant watering lady, but a sauntering, lay back, blue suitor with a cup of coffee in his hand approached me. Off we slowly rambled to meet the investment people.

His demeanor was so lackadaisical that, before we had gone down the third hallway, I was trying to recollect how many shares of IBM stock I still owned, because the thought clearly struck me that this would be a great time to sell it short.

Just one little signal. No sense of urgency in an upper ranking executive. I couldn't believe the difference from the IBM I knew.

Two months later the CEO, was terminated and in came Gerstner. You know the rest of the story.

When that sense of urgency trot with your people slows to a saunter, it's time for lunch!

Multi-Tasking Mary

Some people make a profession out of multi-tasking. They're usually from New York or California. Must be a coastal thing.

There are good and bad times and places for multi-tasking.

Multi-tasking is best done when one is alone, because if you are with someone else or several others, you insult the hell out of them.

The arrogance of thinking they don't know or don't care just doesn't fly.

Speaking of flying. I think a private pilot, while alone, making an IRF (instrument) landing approach at a large heavily-trafficked airport in stormy weather with minimum visibility displays the epitome of a person multi tasking.

It's hands, feet, eyes, ears, and voice all at the same time, and their ain't no room for error. No "awe, shucks, I didn't read the heading right, cause approach control was talking to me and the crosswind was putting me off course, and I couldn't see the runway."

Man you just multi-task or else! I know because I've been there, but hell I'm still here so far!

But if you are on the phone with anyone you respect and at the same time you are catching up with your e-mail, forget about it!

They know, and they are pissed even if they don't say so. And if you don't care; then forget about being a successful entrepreneur.

When I feel someone is doing that to me, I just suddenly stop talking. You'd be amazed at how long the silence goes on. They obviously aren't with me and feel that e-mail is either more important or that they think they can fool me into thinking they are listening to what I am saying. I usually say, when they come back to my multi, that I can call them back if this is a bad time.

Invariably successful leaders and managers are totally focused on what they are doing. That's why they are successful.

I have never talked on the phone to someone I feel is successful that I have not noticed how totally we are focused on the now with our conversation. Notice it sometime!

Those who have to publicly multi task aren't going anywhere. They probably talk on cell phones in restaurants and in the rest rooms!

We need rules, civility codes, and multi-tasking punishment public racking areas where we can throw double whoppers at multi-taskers and award triple mileage to those get direct hits.

Meetings Maven Marvin

In most large companies many people bitch about how there are too many meetings.

It's usually true.

But a fairly consistent truism about the meeting subject is that good leaders try to cut back on the number of meetings and the incompetent leaders try to have more.

Let me tell you about a situation that absolutely sent me into stitches.

I was having one of those one-on-one lunches in my office. This time it was a senior quality control line supervisor.

After a few minutes I brought up the fact that QC seemed to be deteriorating and asked if she had any ideas about what we could do. At first she hesitated. Then she said, "You know, I know all kinds of people have told you things in these one-on-one lunches you have, and I have to tell you, you've never compromised anybody, so can I tell you a story."

Since this was years ago, I can now tell her short story.

Seems her manager was a meeting maven. Any time something went wrong, he would have a meeting. He was convinced that meetings were the cure-all for all problems.

There was one particular recurring problem on Ulanda's line so he called the QC people in again and started yelling about the fact that nothing was

187

being done about this QC problem and he wanted to know now! What the hell is the problem? Where is everybody? Asleep?

That's when one brave now-former employee said. "we're not asleep, we're always in meetings.

You get the picture. Don't let it happen!

PART NINE

STRATEGY IMPERATIVES

As you know, this book is focused on the best management techniques for an entrepreneur to practice while running a fast growing start-up.

However there are challenges, beyond managing people, that an entrepreneur confronts while building a business.

So, while this book stays focused on managing, I will briefly cover the important subjects of strategy and raising money. These two subjects, are as worthy of a separate book as this book is to managing.

Nag vs. Thoroughbred

Business judgment is the capability to distinguish between a
viable and non-viable business based on a fundamental
comprehension of how enterprises compete and make money

Obviously people cannot say they have a successful strategy until they have a success. So it may be helpful for you to review a checklist of the generic qualities which have distinguished successful companies from companies that have been unsuccessful.

GE figured it out for us and teaches it at Crotonville, New York now called the Jack Welch School of Management.

What they discovered is that no matter how well you manage a company, if the strategy is flawed, you will always have problems.

They would take some of their best business unit mangers and throw them at their problem business units, usually to no avail.

The following sentence is critical to your success because if any part of it doesn't work, your chances of making a success of your business diminish substantially.

You must be able to make or buy your product or service at a cost, and sell it at a price that at your projected volume you can make a decent profit while; serving customers who will be satisfied.

191

If you miss your cost, price, or volume targets you, are in deep water without a paddle. That's why the strategy subject is another book. This is meant to be an overview to help stimulate your thinking.

Successful entrepreneurs seem to have an innate sense of understanding what combination of price, cost, and market-place realistically blend together to make a profitable business.

All of the management practices mentioned in this book can help you immeasurably if your strategy turns out to be basically valid. However, if you have a flawed business strategy, it is terribly difficult to turn the nag into a thoroughbred.

Now, you may ask, exactly what are some of the characteristics of that flawed business strategy?

Well, let me give you a check list so that you can test your business idea against proven and well-documented facts about the generic make up of successful businesses.

When I first saw this analysis I thought "Kee-rist" that nag description is my business if I ever saw it! Then I thought, with my perpetually unquenchable optimism, that maybe I could turn it into a Tennessee Trotter!

Here is the difference, so test for yourself.

Nag	**Thoroughbred**
Low cost of entry	High cost of entry
Price sensitive	Price stable
Labor intensive	Low labor requirement
Capital expenditure intensive	Low capital requirement
Low gross margin	High gross margin potential
Raw material sensitive	Little or no raw material required
Commodity product orientation	Proprietary product
No chance of market domination	Good chance at high share

You begin to get the point here.

If the business that you are thinking about starting or the one that you are now running, has all left-column characteristics, think long and hard about how much risk you can handle.

There are ways to make these nag businesses somewhat successful, but it requires intense concentration on the core disciplines mentioned earlier in this book; like focus, forget the frills, be nimble, lean and mean, manage the assets, and on and on.

I know it can be done because I've ridden a nag; could barely get it to trot!

It's much less stressful and more profitable to manage a right-hand-column business. Those thoroughbred opportunities come along once in awhile, but being realistic, they usually take tons of start up money.

Anyway, use the check list, it may at least help you understand what your problems and opportunities may be.

The Cure For Which There is No Disease

The unshakeable belief that you can do anything
is a solid cornerstone for disaster

As mentioned earlier, one of the four major reasons for failure is a flawed strategy.

If you are a new business the first exercise you need to go through, right after sanity checking your business concept against the nag/thoroughbred list, is to be as sure as you can that there is a need or you can create a need for your product or service.

Remember, you must also be able to sell the service at a price that will make a profit., and even more importantly, a price that bring you a profit that results in a successful or more-than-successful return on investment. (ROI).

If you are managing an existing business you have to deal with what you have, but you should use the Nag/Thoroughbred table to see where you can work on improving your strategy.

If you are a student of business history you may remember the following examples of a flawed understanding of the marketplace. All of them failed.

The Avanti, Kaiser, DeLorean and Tucker were all cars produced by well-intentioned entrepreneurs who each had the unbelievable capability to persuade others that his idea was ready and ripe for the consumer of his time.

The capability to produce these advanced cars was only limited by the imagination of creative designers and engineers. Because they were beautiful and unique the powers to be in each case thought the public would create a clamor for them. But it turned out, for one reason or another, the public was just not ready.

About 15 years after these new car introduction failed, another similar but entirely different phenomenon occurred.

This time it wasn't a bunch of creative car designers. This time one very brilliant Englishman took something called the Internet that was primarily a military, scientific, education tool and invented something called the hyperlink protocol.

Tim Berners-Lee, a Cambridge University student studying at the CERN labs in Switzerland, literally revolutionized the business world without planning to or even knowing his tool would create the unbelievable opportunities that followed his introduction of HTTP, the protocol of the World Wide Web

Without it, it seems we'd still all be living in caves eating fleas and trying to light a fire!

The problem became that a whole bunch of risk-taking entrepreneurs and venture capitalist techies in the land of seeds, beads and sandals were bright enough to see the business potential uses for the URL addresses that the protocol made possible, but not bright enough to see that few consumers had any knowledge, know how, inclination or up to date computer goodies.

The challenge was so great however, that they had to give up surfing, skiing, boofing and bofing, long enough to spend tens of billions of others people's money before it became clear that they were just like the previous generation of auto designers.

There was no demand. They were ahead of the curve. They had a cure for which there was no disease.

People didn't need or want it, or know how, in any case, they didn't buy pet food over the Internet.

What really happened was that while the back end of the Internet technology was ready, the front end, which included the need for high speed transmission, low-cost PCs and computer literate consumers, was not in place.

Sort of like a bunch of flight engineers starting a passenger airline two years after the Wright brothers first flight!

Always step back with any idea you have and test to be sure you're not starting a company that offers a service for which there is not yet a need.

There have been many companies and or product lines started based on the premise of what a business person, scientist or technologist knows can be produced without the basic understanding of whether people want the product or service.

One reason for failures is the fact that many times the budding entrepreneur is an engineer, scientist, or technologist whose background, education, inclination and pre- dispositions are not marketing.

If you have an idea and you did not come from the marketing side of business, get help. Test, survey, poll.

Do not ask your friends for they rarely will tell you the truth. They admire you and don't want to hurt you if they think your idea is whacko. Ever tell a friend he or she have an ugly baby?

If you believe strongly that you can create a need for your product or service, then raise eight times more money than you think you will need to get to break-even. It will take that kind of multiple.

If you can't raise that kind of money, and few can, then do what other successful entrepreneurs have done who have created a need for their products.

Start small and prove the concept.

Ray Kroc, founder of McDonalds, started with one burger stand, which he purchased when he saw how well the founders were doing. Then he opened one more, then another and finally he was off and running.

Starbucks, Kinko's, Mail Box Etc, Home Depot, and Walmart are just a few example of entrepreneurs who started small, created or fulfilled a need, and became successful.

Start small, prove the concept, and you too can make a fortune!

PART TEN

RAISING MONEY

How much money do you need to successfully start and run a new company, or build your existing company, and where do you get the money?

This chapter is about how to raise the money for your start-up. It also applies to how you may want to raise more money once you are in business and find you need additional working capital.

This chapter is not about how you determine how much you need. That determination depends on too many individual factors. Your capital expenditure and cash flow forecasts through break-even will tell you how much you need.

If you need less than $30,000 to start up and get to break-even, your source is friends, family and personal loans.

Venture capital won't touch it.

If you need $30,000 to $200,000, it's too much for friends and family and too little for venture capitalists.

Over $200,000, but preferably $500,000 on up to millions is a professional investors game.

The following ideas concern how to structure your deal once you have found investors.

Where you get your money is an entirely different subject, and is not part of this book on managing a company. However they are the revelation of lessons learned the hard way over years of difficult victories and defeats on the field of financing on the part of this entrepreneur.

Financing Comments

Almost every entrepreneur I've ever met wants to start a company and keep control of the majority of the companies stock. This as a rule means 51 percent.

Controlling interest is a noble and practical objective. Who wants one of those aggressive VCs to have a bad day and decide you're not their prince any longer.

Let me tell you something, from our side, the entrepreneurial side.

The last thing that investors or a bank wants to do is run a business.

In fact most don't even know how to run a business. Believe me. I have worked with and for them. Business is a people business and investing is a numbers business. They are numbers people. They realize all of this, so they rely strongly on investing in companies with good management.

So if you're good at management, rest at ease. If you're not, insist on 51 percent.

All of this being said, there are ways for you to have effective control with out having 51 percent of the common stock.

Here are a few things to think about. I am just giving you ideas because each situation is different. But it's best if you know how many tools you have so you can choose the right one, or combination of correct ones.

If you can afford it, you should really discuss these choices with a business professional. Lawyers, accountants and investment bankers who specialize in mergers, acquisitions, buy-outs or start-ups are available although sometimes hard to find, and expensive when found.

Here are some ideas on how to get and keep as much equity as possible.

Letter of Intent from prospective customers

I used these to start my first business. They were extremely helpful in securing both investors and a bank loan. It also helped with not getting my ownership diluted as badly as it might have been for a 27 year old with no start-up experience.

I didn't solicit investors or a loan until I had three "Letters of Intent to Buy" in my quivering hands. The business was B-to-B so that it was easier and more credible to get Letters of Intent from another business than it would have been to get a bunch of letters from consumer prospects.

I wrote the totally non-binding letters myself and asked purchasing managers at All State, International Harvester, and Harris Trust to sign them, which to my total amazement, they did!

They also became my first customers and stayed customers for years.

You can believe how much better a bank and investors felt when I approached them with these LOIs. Once I learned the lingo, I became even more dangerous. Some investors even believed I knew what I was talking about!

Separate and Conquer

Sometimes you just have to give up on the quest for the control.

Hey, thirty-three percent of something may be a hell of a lot better than 51 percent of nothing!

Don't forget though, that if you are looking for control, there are many ways to filet the fish. For instance you can take thirty-three percent but be sure that no other person or entity has more thirty-three percent. That means you and one or two others can control the company.

You can have Class A voting stock and Class B non-voting

You can have Preferred and Common stock.

You can have convertible debentures, which allows your investors to receive fairly high interest on their investment until such time that they decide to convert to stock at some pre-determined price. Or they may opt not to convert and just be paid back. It gives them a good look-see at your performance promises.

It's obvious that you will need the advice of pros on investing and legal issues to help you. I'm just throwing out ideas here in the hope that a little knowledge can go a long way for you.

Claw Back

This is a hell of a term. You can see it comes from the trenches of some pretty tough professionals. One way to get 51 percent if your investors don't want you to have it at first is to give up and go to a lesser amount.

But have a claw back clause that allows you to go up to 51 percent if you meet certain objectives.

The objectives in this case may not be profit objectives, but rather some achievement such as the number of customers or a certain sales volume that your investors feel is important to achieve.

There are many aspects of this and it negotiation intensive, but it is a tool.

Earn Out

In this case you again take less than 51 percent.. However, if the company earns a pre-negotiated amount of money over a negotiated period of time, you increase your percentage ownership.

It is somewhat like a claw back, but it's based purely on profit performance. Again, this is negotiation intensive and has to be a win-win for all.

Warrants

These can be awarded to you in a way that allows you to exercise them at some later date, which in effect increases your equity in the firm. The tax and legal implications change all the time, so you must see a business pro on this.

Options

These are similar to warrants only with these you can exercise the options at pre-determined times. Most likely you have to pay the option price at the time you exercise them. This also allows you to increase your equity stake.

The percentage of ownership of the company that is usually given to a CEO or founder in options can range from as low as 6 percent to as high as 12 percent of the company. Find out what the parameters are in your industry before you negotiate the options.

Salary and Bonus

If you are not entirely satisfied with your percentage of ownership, then you can negotiate a more than comfortable base salary and a bonus structure that may contain more than just one achievement benchmark. Again, this depends on you and your investors and is only limited by your imagination. Just remember it is futile to negotiate anything other than on a win-win basis.

Cash Comments

First, until you are solidly profitable for at least six quarters you will most likely always need more cash in reserve than you ever planned on. If your business is seasonal, it will be longer.

Second, since the above is true, be sure you raise enough cash to take you through this period.

Third, if you are surprisingly successful you can outrun your cash quickly.

That is one reason why I have emphasized over and over the need for a good accounting department and a good controller.

You have to control your growth to your cash flow or take a breather and re-finance.

Fourth, cash can be squandered or generated from all kinds of places right within the company. Aggressive and disciplined accounts receivable and inventory management harbor money.

Lax management in these two areas can sink you.

Fifth, as a last resort, a large, willing supplier can extend credit for a limited amount of time until you solve your cash problem. This can be in the form of extended payables or a loan. They will not do it unless they see your plan to pay them back. This is risky, but has happened many more times than one might think.

Sixth, you can finance your receivables with receivables financing firms like GE capital. If you have financially stable customers you can borrow up to 80 percent on the money they owe you and then pay back the financing company when you collect the receivables.

Receivables financing is expensive and can be a sink-hole trap that is difficult to get out from under. It is a last resort, but it has helped many companies survive.

It's better to give up some equity for additional financing, but sometimes that isn't a choice. You wouldn't be an entrepreneur if you were risk averse, would you?

PART ELEVEN

IS ENTREPRENEURSHIP REALLY FOR ME?

Before you even start, be sure entrepreneurship is for you.

Most entrepreneurs don't even think about it; they just want to do it.

But I do believe you should take a deep breath, let the testosterone or estrogen settle for a moment, take a yellow pad, sit down, for ten minutes (I know that's a long time for an entrepreneur to sit down), and write why you should, and why you should not embark on an adventure in entrepreneurship.

Because deciding on a career as an entrepreneur is such an important decision I have created a questionnaire for you.

Answer the questions honestly and then check your score. The result will speak for itself.

1. Risk   Score1-10_____

You have to be comfortable with risk. There is no way it makes sense to embark on a venture and then lose sleep every night. Sometimes, yes, but we all need sleep and most risk takers don't lose too much sleep, risk is in their genes.

If you are risk averse, take a good job, with good benefits, with a good company, and life will be much happier. Plus, if you really have what it takes, you may rise to be the top dog in a bigger and more secure company.

2. Independence   Score1-10_____

You have to be truly independent; and enjoy it. And be comfortable with it. There will be many times when you see others, competitors in and out of your industry, all following the same path. That path or practice may not be the best for you and your company. You can't be a lemming. You must be independent enough to do what you think is correct, even if you are out of synch with the others.

The entrepreneurial life, by its nature, is not a collegial one. You are not using the advantages of the form if you can't make decisions quickly and decisively. It's one of the many advantages you have over bureaucratic competitors, and you must have an independent spirit to use it.

3. Self Confidence   Score1-10_____

Almost all successful people are self-confidant; but an entrepreneur has to be supremely self-confidant. Not cocky, but deeply confident.

Most confidence comes from storing knowledge and applying your own logic links to it. It isn't puffery, it's a deep-down sense of calmness, and most people sense it in you. You can't fake it.

It's also as much about knowing what you can't do as well as what you can do.

4. A need to run the show   Score1-10_____

Are you known as a control freak? Most entrepreneurs start their own business to fill the need to make things happen the way they want them to happen. Sometimes this need is even more important than the desire to make money.

There is certainly nothing wrong with the tendency, as long as it's tempered with a semi-balanced approach to listen to two sides of a problem.

You can't and don't know everything.

5. Decisiveness   Score1-10_____

You know whether you are good at decisions. Do you prefer committees and study groups? Yes, you need all the facts to make a good decision, but you're never going to get them all! When do you have the reasonable amount that allows you to make a reasonable decision?

Remember one thing, a really good decision will only be known to be good at a future point in time, and that will be called good judgment, one of the most valuable of all qualities.

6. Challenge orientation   Score1-10_____

It is obvious that continually facing challenges comes with the turf. If you like things settled down, orderly, and everything in place, forget about an adventure into entrepreneurship. It will be years before you control your daily life. If ever!

.

7. Energy   Score1-10_____

You have to have an over-active pituitary or an excess abundance of red blood cells. This is not the track for a low-level Type B. You can't even utter the word "tired" or you will be laughed out by all those A types you've hired. You know yourself on this one, so don't fudge the score!

8. Persuasiveness   Score1-10_____

There is no way you can be successful as an entrepreneur without an abundance of this quality. You have to convince people to work for you when they have many more secure options. You have to convince people to invest in you when they are full of doubt about you, your track record, and most of all, your cockamamie idea.

They will look to see if you have every one of the above qualities, and they will "devil's advocate" your idea until you feel like telling them to take a hike.

9. Passion   Score1-10_____

This is not only a quality you need, and lots of it, but also the one you need to look for in anyone you hire. Lackadaisical people do not have a place in an entrepreneurial environment. As the leader of your endeavor, your enthusiasm has to be real, and if it is, it will become contagious.

10. Creativity   Score1-10_____

Creativity, it seems, is most often associated with artists, writers and inventors. The creation of a business is a process that in many ways is similar. You start with a rough plan, and once underway, you are constantly changing and adjusting the creation as you learn and improve. However, unlike an artist or writer who must in some short order finish the process and be done with it, the entrepreneur takes years and years, and still never seems to finish the creation. Those creative juices have to keep flowing, so there better be an abundant supply.

11. Courage   Score1-10_____

It takes courage to follow an independent path. It takes courage to see it the way it is when it's not the way you wanted it to be. It takes courage to tell it the way it is, to shareholders, banks and employees. But the courage to do these things will always pay off. If you can't practice this kind of courage you will have a difficult time indeed.

12. Candor   Score1-10_____

Truthfulness becomes a linchpin for all you do at your company. Your people can see it and will admire it. Your suppliers, customers and investors all will appreciate it and come to depend on it. It will carry you far. You will need the goodwill of it when you are wrong. And we all are wrong sometimes. Changing paths when it is evident you are pursuing a wrong direction, one you have ardently espoused, takes candor and courage.

OK, you've taken the test and added up your score.
There are 12 questions. So the highest score you can score is **120**.
The lowest is **0**.

Score results:

12 to 48

You should throw this book in the trash and get back to your job.

49 to 72

When you go back to work, ask for a staff or research position.

73 to 84

Ask your boss if you can head up the next new product or service offering.

85 to 108

Write a short business plan for your idea, run the first year numbers by month and see where the break-even is. Then go to family and friends for some first stage money.

109 to 120

You've already second mortgaged your house, and you'll probably be successful, just don't get carried away. Keep the costs down, stay close to the prospects and customers, get rid of the non-performers, focus, measure, and sell.

It's going to be one hell of a ride, and you are going to enjoy it.

PART TWELVE

CROSSING THE BRIDGE

This book has consolidated all the things this entrepreneur has learned about effectively managing a start-up through to a successfully growing business

We have discussed management practices with an emphasis on the importance of people as the single most important asset.

And very importantly, we have discussed the practices you need to follow to be a successful entrepreneur and manager.

We've also touched on strategy, raising money, and structuring your company.

We have not discussed what your idea is. We cannot do that here because it is an intensely individual thing.

I have tried to give you a frame work against which you can test yourself and your idea so that you will improve your chances for success.

Only you know whether you feel you are up to the task of hiring and managing people successfully.

If you have not yet started your business, let me share something with you.

I have been an entrepreneur and growing company manager for many years, and because I have spoken at conferences and generally made myself decently available to those interested in entrepreneurship, I have found that there is one over-riding problem with many who wish to start a company.

They talk about it to everyone, and think about it, and talk about it; but the biggest failing is that they will not "Cross the Bridge." I even have given talks on just this one subject: "Crossing the Bridge."

Talk is easy. Mustering the courage to actually start the business is extremely difficult. There is substantial risk. There is the wife, the children, the mortgage, and on it goes. That's why I have the Quiz on entrepreneurship. Don't start a company if you haven't passed the quiz.

If you have passed and are still talking.

Stop.

Cross the Bridge.

You'll feel much better and I would hope the following from Teddy Roosevelt will convince you.

THE MEASURE OF LIFE

It is not the critic who counts, nor the man who points out how the strong man stumbles, or where the doer of deeds could have done better.

The credit belongs to the man who is actually in the arena; whose face is marred by dust and sweat; who strives valiantly; who errs and may fail again, because there is no effort without error or shortcoming; but he who actually strives to do the deeds, who does know the great enthusiasm, the great devotion, who spends himself in a worthy cause, at best, knows in the end the triumph of high achievement, and at the worst, if he fails, at least fails while daring greatly, so that his place shall never be with those cold and timid soles who know neither victory or defeat.

—Teddy Roosevelt